IBN AL-BALAD

A CONCEPT OF EGYPTIAN IDENTITY

SOCIAL, ECONOMIC AND POLITICAL
STUDIES OF THE MIDDLE EAST

ÉTUDES SOCIALES, ÉCONOMIQUES ET
POLITIQUES DU MOYEN ORIENT

VOLUME XXIV

SAWSAN EL-MESSIRI

IBN AL-BALAD

A CONCEPT OF EGYPTIAN IDENTITY

LEIDEN
E. J. BRILL
1978

IBN AL-BALAD

A CONCEPT OF EGYPTIAN IDENTITY

BY

SAWSAN EL-MESSIRI

LEIDEN
E. J. BRILL
1978

Le but de la collection est de faciliter la communication entre le grand public international et les spécialistes des sciences sociales étudiant le Moyen-Orient, et notamment ceux qui y résident. Les ouvrages sélectionnés porteront sur les phénomènes et problèmes contemporains: sociaux, culturels, économiques et administratifs. Leurs principales orientations relèveront de la théorie générale, des problématiques plus précises, et de la politologie: aménagement des institutions et administration des affaires publiques.

The series is designed to serve as a link between the international reading public and social scientists studying the contemporary Middle East, notably those living in the area. Works to be included will be characterized by their relevance to actual phenomena and problems: whether social, cultural, economic political or administrative. They will be theory-oriented, problem-oriented or policy-oriented.

ISBN 90 04 05664 5

PRINTED IN THE NETHERLANDS

To my children,
Wafaa', Mahmoud, Do'aa and Hamada.

May their search for an Egyptian
identity be more authentic than ours.

TABLE OF CONTENTS

FOREWORD

Sawsan El-Messiri's book is important; and it has a great deal of charm without in the least abandoning the highest scholarly standards. Its charm and its significance are connected. They are intimately linked to its subject matter. The book might well be subtitled 'a study in populism'. It is a study in the culture and self-image – and, indeed, outward image – of the Egyptian urban *folk*, of what the French semi-pejoratively call *peuple*.

The poor are always with us, they used to say: ordinary people, as distinct from the elite, have always existed. But folk culture has acquired a special significance in modern times. Modern society is occupationally mobile, it presupposes universal education and literacy, it requires its citizens to be capable of rapid, effective and reasonably precise communication with strangers. Indeed, encountering "strangers," i.e. non-acquaintances, is no longer a rare event, as the meeting of the pilgrim, fugitive or wandering peddler used to be; it is part and parcel of daily work and leisure. This being so, what is required is that citizens who must so often meet each other for the first time should, more or less, share the same culture. Their familiarity with each other can no longer spring from long personal acquaintance and intimacy, but only from sharing the same culture. But *which* culture?

At the start of that process of homogenisation which seems so inescapable in our time, there is always a number of rival claimants to the status of the newly pervasive and dominant culture. Is it to be the idiom of some ruling stratum, or the language of the new technology, or what?

Anthropologists have spoken of the contrast or conflict between the Great Tradition and its folk rival, an opposition no doubt inherent in every literate and urban tradition. But the matter is really more complex. In the modern world, there is a whole hierarchy or multiplicity of Great Traditions, and a variety of folk ones, all of them often operating and competing in the same or overlapping areas. The ensuing Kulturkampf has assumed a variety of forms in different parts of the world since the 18th century. It has its distinctive forms within Muslim society, and within Egypt in particular. A number of distinct 'great' or central traditions opposed a variety of popular ones: the religion of urban scholars as against popular saints, towns against tribes, a Mamluk soldiery and bureaucracy against craftsmen and peasants. Following onto this type of opposition, the colonial period brought, successively, a foreign commercial bourgeoisie and alien authorities, followed by a new elite with local origins but an alien culture.

Muslim cities in the past feared tribesmen, and one does not idealise what one fears. Hence the idealisation of the countryman came later or not at all, or was perpetrated vicariously by foreigners. In opposition to foreign culture, nationalism tended in many places to identify with the Local Great tradition and to disavow folk models as corruptions of an ideal past. In Egypt an urban folk culture distinguishes itself both from the erstwhile Muslim but Mamluk rulers, and also from their Westernised successors, and from the countryfolk. It is this distinctive culture which may well set the future tone in the country.

For the age of nationalism and economic development which we are witnessing is, amongst other things, a period committed to the erosion of this cultural gap: the modernisation of the economy is to be accompanied by the popularisation of the national culture. Henceforth, the idiom of government and economy is to be continuous with that of the people.

This aspiration for cultural unity is a serious and genuine, not merely a nominal endeavour; this aspiration may find an authentic fulfilment in the culture which is attaining self-consciousness under the name of *ibn al-balad*. In a country such as Egypt, a crucial element in the new national culture must inevitably be that of its large urban masses. Sawsan El-Messiri has investigated, analysed and described the urban folk culture of Egypt with sensitivity, sympathy, humour and insight, with scholarship but without pedantry, with familiarity devoid of condescension. She tells us how this culture appears both to outsiders and to those who live it, how its self-consciousness crystallised in reaction to successive historic situations, and she explains the political and social attitudes which it engenders. This book will rightly be read for pleasure as well as instruction. Westerners eager to know the feel and texture of Egyptian culture will find in it a worthy and up-to-date successor of the work of Edward Lane. It does a very great deal to illuminate and explain the life, values and ideas of modern Egyptian towns. It is far more than merely descriptive: it helps us to understand better the changes currently taking place in Egyptian society.

Ernest Gellner
Professor
Fellow of the British Academy

ACKNOWLEDGMENTS

From original conception to completion, the present work has passed through several stages, benefitting from the support, encouragement and criticism of friends and colleagues too numerous to thank individually. For its initial stages I would like to thank in particular Laila al-Hamamsy, Mardson Jones, Cynthia Nelson, John Waterbury and Elizabeth Taylor. To all of those who helped me in this work, my debt cannot be adequately expressed; each one will perhaps recognize the trace of his or her guiding hand in the following pages.

While it is only natural for academic pursuits to be influenced by a concern for one's own society, so much more was the attraction for the *awlād al-balad* in the aftermath of the June 1967 war. Since that time, this work has grown out of a master's thesis at the American University in Cairo through continued contact with and research among this segment of the Cairene population. Only a modest tribute can be paid here to a few who have seen the manuscript through its final stage. Talal Asad read the whole work in successive drafts offering valuable comments and suggestions, never failing in his warm encouragement. Amidst her other duties, Linda Bacon found the time to edit and type portions of the manuscript. Diana De Treville read the whole manuscript and made useful comments. Ernest Gellner will, I trust, not take it amiss, if a "client" expresses her gratitude to a "patron". David Waines made unremitting efforts to improve the quality of the text but must be absolved from any shortcomings which remain; these are the author's responsibility alone.

Finally, my greatest debt is to the *awlād al-balad* who not only extended to me their full cooperation and tolerated my intrusion into their lives, but also generously accepted me as one of their community. To them I owe a greater understanding of my own identity as an Egyptian.

INTRODUCTION

This study is an essay on the concept of *ibn al-balad** in Egyptian society and culture. It is concerned with the social manifestations of the groups associated with the concept in both historical and contemporary times. *Ibn al-balad* as a linguistic term seems to have as many meanings as there are social situations. Anyone who visits Egypt is bound to hear the term and its derivatives usually used in such contexts as: "He is an *ibn al-balad*", "we are *awlād al-balad,*" "we are like each other *awlād al-balad*," "she is a *bint al-balad*", "that is *baladī*" and so forth. The epithet *ibn al-balad* has no precise equivalent in English and therefore to accept only its literal meaning would be misleading because the phrase conveys nuances that are perhaps understood best in specific contexts. The sentence *"huwwa ibn al-balad,"* for example, means literally "he is a son of the country." However, in every-day usage it can have a variety of referents, such as a person who is usually dressed in a *gallābiyya* (flowing gown), or who comes from a *baladī* (popular) quarter, or someone who cannot be hoodwinked, or one who is never punctual, or one who is knowledgeable about folk traditions.

In some contexts *ibn al-balad* is employed by Egyptians to refer to themselves as Egyptians. In this use the word seems to be synonymous with the term *miṣrī* (Egyptian). This is only exceptionally the case, for in other contexts it is clear that while an *ibn al-balad* is always an Egyptian, not all Egyptians are *awlād al-balad;* Egyptian nationality is necessary but not sufficient to identify one as an *ibn al-balad.* Egyptians who are known to have foreign ancestry, even two or three generations back, are not considered *awlād al-balad,* but *khawagāt*[1] (foreigners). What then, aside from ancestry and nationality, makes a "real" Egyptian? There seem to be certain characteristics and attributes that differentiate a "real" Egyptian, an

---

* *Ibn* (pl. *awlād*) literally means "son", *bint* (pl. *banāt*) means "daughter". *Balad* is an ambiguous term used to denote a locality of any size, as big as Egypt or as small as any village. *Baladī* is an adjective derived from *balad.*

[1] *Khawāga* literally means any western foreigner, but in Egyptian colloquial Arabic, it implies "an outsider", in contrast to *awlād al-balad*, who are indigenous. *Khoga*, a linguistic root in Classical Arabic, also meant "teacher", but one who taught subjects other than the Qur'ān. It came to be applied to Copts, who were often teachers and were occasionally associated with western foreigners by virtue of their Christian background and earlier political and economic ties with foreigners. The subtle ramifications of this important contrast of *khawāga* and *ibn al-balad* will become clearer in later chapters.

ibn al-balad, not only from any foreigner, but from other Egyptians as well. An obvious and typical characteristic of the "real" Egyptian is his use of his mother tongue. The *ibn al-balad* speaks Arabic in the local Egyptian dialect and not "broken Arabic." If an Egyptian does not master his mother tongue, which has happened often enough as a result of westernization, foreign occupation and the emphasis on foreign eduction, he may be referred to sarcastically as a *khawāga.*

Gaiety, good humor mixed with sarcasm and cynicism, and a tendency to live for the moment are considered by Egyptians to be typical attributes of the "real" Egyptians, traits indeed which seem to have been outstanding since earlier times. Writers and historians have often referred to the same qualities. For example Abū'l-Salt[2] the historian (1067 A.D.) said that the Egyptian character is dominated by a desire for sensuous pleasures and recreation as well as gaiety and amiability. Further, that these features are more pronounced in their character than they are in any other group which he had observed. When Ibn Khaldūn first came to Egypt he stated that the Egyptians lack foresight because he did not find them storing food, as was the custom in other countries, but rather buying their food twice a day, in the morning and at night. However, Aḥmed Amīn comments that it is their lack of foresight which allows them to be gay and jolly, and that if people do not think of consequences they will not worry, and thus the possibilities for joking are increased. He also observed that in his days (1900–1950) the most miserable people who lived in the worst conditions and had the least money were the most jolly. Thus, in *baladī* (popular) coffee-houses, unemployed workers and artisans would sit about in circles joking. He found that joking was a very prominent feature of social intercourse and entertainment and that wit was loved and appreciated. Egyptians love jokes and some of them follow the latest joke as they would the latest news or prices of cotton. This concern for jokes and joking is more common in Cairo than other Egyptian towns and villages (Amin 1953).

In many Egyptian circles it is often pointed out that this sense of humor is a kind of outlet for the frustrations the Egyptians have experienced during foreign occupations. Hāmid 'Ammār, an Egyptian social anthropologist, points to a similar interpretation in the following terms:

> The joke became a characteristic of the Egyptian pattern. It seems that the joke is used (by an Egyptian) to satisfy his internal feelings and comfort those who hear it. It also keeps him away from the

[2] Abu'l-Salt Umayya, born in 460/1067 in Donia (Daniya) in the Levante. About 489/1096 we find him in Alexandria and Cairo where he continued to pursue his studies. In *al-Rasā'il al-Misriyya* he gives vivid information about the affairs and customs of Egypt. (The Encyclopedia of Islam, Vol. I, p. 149).

> (serious) subject, and even from reality itself. Hence, many of the clever Egyptian jokes act as release for the political and social frustrations that afflict the people. They also act as an escape from anxieties and hence make life bearable (Ammār 1964:83).

Other characteristics regarded as typical of the "real" Egyptian include simplicity and goodness. The *ibn al-balad* conceives of himself as essentially good and he believes that this a result of living off the "good earth"[3], an earth generous in providing him with his needs and that would never fail him. As often commented, goodness is "the soil of our country". In turn, the "real" Egyptian must be loyal to his country, love it and remain attached to it; unless a man is patriotic, he is not identified as a true *ibn al-balad*. The *ibn al-balad* also sees himself as being direct and simple in speech, not sophisticated. It is often said in conversation, when someone starts to philosophize and use classical Arabic words, "Make your point in *baladī*". Likewise, when a doctor starts to explain to a family a patient's condition using medical expressions, he may be told: "explain the case again in *baladī*", meaning, say clearly and simply what you want to say.

The "real" Egyptian (i.e. *ibn al-balad*) is seen as having a "fatalistic" attitude towards life. Respondents described his way of living from day to day, heedless of the morrow, as due to the *ibn al-balad's* belief that tomorrow is unpredictable. Fate can interfere at any time and change one's plans; hence, it is useless to make plans. Perhaps this philosophy is best expressed in the phrase *"in shā' Allah"* (literally, "if God wills"), which is attached to virtually every expression of intent, or those relating to the future.

The concept implies that *ibn al-balad* lives from day to day and that he regards whatever wealth he accumulates in his life as worthless, since "no one takes anything with him when he dies".[4] This is a common saying, often directed at those who appear to plan their lives carefully. Material things are seen as of limited value since they do not assure success in the after-life. It is rather a man's good actions that count. As another saying puts it: "None but the good action will remain to be counted for you in the after-life." Such attitudes must by no means be confused with an advocacy of asceticism or self-denial.

---

[3] The good earth here refers to Egypt. Egyptians usually refer to Egypt as the country of goods or our country which is abundant with goods. *Ibn al-balad* is not primarily rural. The historical precedents for this misconception will be dealt with in Chapter 1 as with the more specific differentiations between him and the "*fallāḥ*" (peasant) in Chapter 2 and 3. Here the meaning verges on the metaphorical, like "the salt of the earth".

[4] An interesting contrast would be the "Protestant Ethic" of the industrialized West. Both of these conceptions of fate can be compatible with either conservative or radical political persuasions, but are traditionally rooted in religious teachings that have numerous social ramifications.

In the folklore the concept relates to the Egyptian masses but more specifically to the Cairene folk. Whereas in villages the *fallāḥīn* (the peasantry), which comprise a vast majority of the Egyptian masses, could identify themselves as *awlād al-balad*, historically it was the Cairenes who were identified as *awlād al-balad*. From the mid-thirteenth century Egypt was dominated in succession by Mamlukes and Ottomans, for a brief interval by the French, then by Muḥammad 'Alī's regime and later by his descendents under British tutelage. It was in the face of these alien Cairo-based elements that the indigenous inhabitant sought to perserve and assert his particular identity. It is scarcely surprising that manifestations of such a cultural confrontation should occur in Cairo, and that the concept of *ibn al-balad* would imply a Cairene, since Cairo and Egypt have always been identified in Egyptian consciousness with the same word, "*miṣr*." In addition, since a large percentage of the population resides in Cairo, the masses have traditionally been more sensitive to the authoritarian measures of the foreign ruling elite as a result of their closer contacts with them.

Historically the folk characters of Cairo were identified as *al-shuṭṭār, al-'uyyār, al-'uyyāq, al-zu'r and al-futūwāt.*[5] In the folk literature of the *siyar*[6] (biographies) these characters symbolized the oppressed Cairene masses and their reaction to their condition. The literature depicts them as

---

[5] *al-Shutttār*: literally means the clever, *al-'uyyār*: the thieves, *al-'uyyāq* whose root is *'ā'iq*: meaning an obstacle, i.e. those who block the road, implying highwaymen. These *'uyyāq* were characterized by their extra neatness and good looks. Now the adjective is used for anyone who is well dressed. *Futūwāt*, derived from *fata* (singular) and *fityān* (plural) literally means youth, but implies gallantry and chivalry. (For more details see Sawsan El-Messiri "The Changing Role of the *Futūwa* in the Social Structure of Cairo", 1977, edited by Gellner and Waterbury). These terms have different connotations in different periods and according to different sources, yet the folk literature has pictured these groups as heroes who possess certain values and mannerisms that reflect the folk's self-image. *Ibn al-balad* as a folk character seems to be an extension of these models. He incorporates the same self-image of these groups. The association of these groups and the *ibn al-balad* type is obvious in the folk tales. (For more details see Yūnis 1969).

[6] *al-siyar:* a specific kind of folk tale that narrates the biographies of certain folk heroes such as Abū Zayd al-Hilālī and al-Zāhir Bibars. Some of these *siyar* deal mainly with folk characters such as *sirat* One Thousand and One Nights, al-Zāhir Bibars and 'Alī al-Zaybaq. Researchers have divided One Thousand and One Nights into four categories. The fourth category of this tale records the role of the professional *shuṭṭār* and *'uyyāq* vis-a-vis the rulers. In *sirat* al-Ẓahir Bibars the groups of *shuṭṭār* and *'uyyāg* are represented as common people who occupy certain professions such as *al-'usṭa* Osman who is a livryman. 'Usta Osman as a folk hero defends and liberates the poor and weak by using his skills as one of the *shuṭṭār*, who are skilled in fighting techniques, as well as in playing pranks on his opponents. In addition to these skills he was considered a holy man. As for 'Alī al-Zaybaq, his biography represents him as an *ibn al-balad* with all his mannerisms and attributes. He was the most highly acclaimed of all the *shuṭṭār*. He is similar to 'Usta Osman except that the folk imagination did not attribute to him any holy characteristics. These particular *siyar* are known for their Cairene setting and hence their characters are Cairene folk heroes. (Yūnis, 1969).

rebel heroes resisting the exploiting foreign elite, protecting the weak and poor, and dispensing justice amongst their people. Prior to the advent of western influence, these folk characters and their exploits served as a source of comfort and a rallying point for the indigenous Egyptians who opposed the foreign ruler. In the face of a foreign ruling elite the indigenous population, for various reasons, became increasingly self-conscious, which enabled them to achieve solidarity to resist this elite.

The first breakdown of this unity came with the forceful attempts to modernize Egyptian society. Muḥammad 'Alī, by laying the foundations of a modern state, abolished many institutions thus undermining the masses' means of resistance. Modernization, accelerating under Muhammad 'Alī (1805–1849), brought with it the gradual Egyptianization of certain sectors of society, hitherto the sole domain of the alien, foreign ruler. For example, modernization required an increasing number of civil servants. Initially, these were found in the higher levels of the bureaucracy selected from among the graduates of Muḥammad 'Alī's and Ismā'īl's (1862-1879) schools and from the many young Egyptians sent to Europe to study. They composed the nucleus of what is called the "*effendi* class"(bureaucrats)[7] and served as a social bridge between the Turkish elite (Ottomans) and the Egyptian masses and lower middle class. The *effendī* class aspired to be part of the upper middle class or what was identified as the *awlād al-zawāt*[8] (upper class persons). In their aspiration to be *awlād al-zawāt* they made continuous efforts to change the symbols of their class, such as, furniture, dress, language and style of life along the lines of the foreign elite. With the narrowing of the gap between the alien ruler and this upward moving Egyptian element there was simultaneously created a growing fissure between the latter and the folk masses. This mobile Egyptian group also absorbed the ruler's contempt for the masses and thereby brought upon themselves the folk's exclusion of them from identification with the *awlād al-balad*.

---

[7] *Effendī:* The word *effendī* is one of the titles of address introduced by the Turks in Egypt, meaning "sir". Among the Turks and during the Turkish rule the term *effendi* used to denote high status. The *walī* and the representative of the Ottoman Empire used to be addressed by this title. It used also to be the title of members of the royal family, *Shaykh al-Islām* and religious judges. Other Turkish titles such as *Pasha* and *Bey* were less prestigious than *effendī.* But later it became the title of the government employees who dress in suits and *tarboush* like the original Turkish rulers (al-Bishri 1939: 22).

[8] In classical Arabic *zawāt* literally denotes "the chief attribute," and is originally used as *zawāt al-ḥaythiya*, i.e. "people of importance." Those who owned a lot of land were people of importance. Hence in colloquial Arabic the term *zawāt* came to designate a rich or aristocratic person. It is also used metaphorically to denote certain attitudes or notions of the Egyptian upper class.

Under the British occupation, from 1882, the processes of westernization and Egyptianization of the ruling and economic structure intensified. The transformation of the Egyptian economy during the nineteenth century and its absorption into the European economic system changed the position of several social groups. First, the European community rapidly increased, representing powerful capitalist interests now under British protection. Second, the growth of a class of Egyptian landed proprietors (identified as *awlād al-zawāt*) occupied an increasingly advantageous position which emerged in direct opposition to the *awlād al-balad*. Third, the emerging Egyptian bureaucrats were replacing the diminishing class of Turco-Circassians, who in turn were becoming more closely assimilated within Egyptian society.

These processes initially resulted in a further isolation and depreciation of the concept of *ibn al-balad,* which symbolized the "real" Egyptian identity, while the emerging *effendī* class succumbed in varying degrees to what they believed the western good life to be. The *ibn al-balad,* on the other hand, was downgraded to the undesirable lower orders. The increasing distance between *awlād al-balad* and the emerging Egyptian bureaucrats is well illustrated by the magazine caricatures of *al-miṣrī effendī* "the true Egyptian" in the late 1920's. He was a typical petty bureaucrat in western suit and Turkish fez. He shared two worlds, the European and the Egyptian, although not completely absorbed in the former and no longer integrated fully into the latter.

Later, with the spread of national consciousness, the image of *al-misrī effendī* came to be felt as an inadequate representation of the true Egyptian. The search for a genuine replacement was intensified after the 1952 revolution with the abolition of the symbols and reality of European occupation and domination together with its Egyptian aristocratic collaboration. Gamāl 'Abdel Nāṣer was seen as the first *"ibn al-balad"* to rule the country, that is, the first Egyptian emerging from his people to govern them. In the years following the revolution there was both a conscious and unconscious effort to revive and strengthen Egyptian culture. This was clearly evident in the development of the arts and literature in which the themes were drawn from day-to-day Egyptian life. Folk art, music and dances also were revived, folk images were glorified and the concept of *ibn al-balad* came to the forefront as the symbol for asserting Egyptian identity.

Thus, *ibn al-balad* as a concept implies various levels of meanings and as a linguistic term is used in numerous contexts. As a member of the society I use the term automatically in specific isolated contexts without noticing the underlying patterns of meaning nor the variation in usages. I first believed that the term applied only to a set of attributes that identify one as an Egyptian. Later, in reviewing the Egyptian folklore, I discovered another layer of meaning which reflects the close association between the concept and the Cairene masses. Further investigation revealed the complexity of the term and the numerous contexts in which it is used. Underlying the variable usage of the term the meaning could be divided into two broad contexts implying (1) meaning referring to behavioral characteristics or norms, (2) meaning referring to a specific group that could denote either the collectivity of Egyptians in general or a specific group of Egyptians. The specific group of Egyptians implied in the concept *ibn al-balad* was articulated differently by different people in different situations and in different periods. To understand these differences, I had to look at the social structure of the society and examine the processes that brought about these changes.

A major analytical problem faced in the research was that no one (to my knowledge) so far had attempted to define the group explicitly. Whether in folklore, histographies, novels, language or socio-cultural analysis, the reality of the collectivity of *awlād al-balad* is only implied. But how would one go about delineating the social reality of the group? To discover this social reality it was necessary to investigate its historical origins, the way other people think of the group and the self-definition of the group itself. To avoid any *a priori* assumption, my approach in this study was to start with the 'common-sense' meanings that the members of the culture share and to get at what Schutz calls the subjective interpretations: "... subjective interpretations of meaning are above all a typification of the common-sense world, the actual way which men in daily life do interpret their own and each other's behavior" (Schutz 1960).

Awlād al-balad as a group are analyzed in part of this research as a typification, i.e. an image that does not conform in all aspects with actual behavior yet is part of the social reality of that group. In some contexts, the typification of *awlād al-balad* became stereotyped. Some groups used it with a "fixed impression which conforms very little to the facts it pretends to represent and results from our defining first and observing second" (Maccoby and Hartley 1958 : 41). It is within the above subjective level of meaning that the concept of *ibn al-balad* is first approached. However this subjective level of meaning is complemented by an objective interpretation. I have attempted to examine the relationship between the subjective reality of a group and how it is associated with certain socio-economic and political structures in the society. I have also attempted to trace the historical transformations of the meaning implied in the concept *ibn al-balad*.

The specific questions raised in this study are: Is there a class or category of Egyptians who are identified within the country as *awlād al-balad?* If so, who are they and what is their role and status in the larger society? In what follows I shall try to describe the actual social groups referred to as *awlād al-balad* in different social situations and periods. I shall begin by an analysis of the historical roots of the concept, then go on to examine other views of the group *awlād al-balad* and finally discuss the self-image of the group itself.

CHAPTER ONE

HISTORICAL DEVELOPMENT OF THE CONCEPT IBN AL-BALAD

In the foregoing introductory survey we have seen the close association between the concept *ibn al-balad* in a very broad, loose sense and the Egyptian identity. More specifically, the term *awlād al-balad* refers to the Cairene masses. The concept *ibn al-balad* does not appear in the literature before the 18th century.[1] Medieval Arabic historical literature, like most western historical works, may be characterized by the total absence of concern for the lives, the fates, fortunes or the minimal conditions of the masses. Their existence is noted by historians usually only in times of crisis, during rebellions and uprisings against authority; in any event, little more than their mere existence as anonymous masses is recorded. Their basic characteristics, therefore, remain largely hidden from the historian's probing searches. One point of interest may be noted here. Whereas some of the historical terms for the masses are neutral such as *al-'āmma* (commoners) others bear more pejorative and specific connotations, such as *al-zu'r* (scoundrels). By contrast, the term *awlād al-balad*, at a primary level of meaning, appears to convey a higher level of prestige for the indigenous masses, being recognized as 'sons of the country' and hence an important group in the life of the whole Egyptian community. Is this change of usage indicative of a change in the actual status of the indigenous population, or is it simply a linguistic whim of historians of the period? The argument here assumes that in the eighteenth and nineteenth centuries a group of the indigenous population was indentified as *awlād al-balad* who had acquired a certain status and power in relation to the ruling foreign population. The main question raised in this chapter is: who were the social groups or classes identified as *awlād al-balad* in this period?

The social classes that appear in the extant literature during the Mamluk period were stratified as follows: a military elite of Mamluks who possessed undisputed power. They were labelled as *al-khāṣṣa* referring to the sultan and his retinue, the highest ranking *amīrs* and the officials. Second in rank were the notables *(al-a'yān),* who theoretically could be recruited from any class or group. They included the high ranking *'ulamā'*, bureaucrats and merchants. In many cases the notables were able to counteract the ruling

[1] In surveying some of the major historical literature of the Mamluk period one does not find the term *ibn al-balad* or its derivatives used. It is only in the eighteenth century that one notices its usage in historical literature.

elite as a coexistent force of power, but by and large notables were committed to the regime and were unable to stand against the monopoly of military power. Last in rank were the masses or lower classes who were identified as *al-'āmma* (common people) as opposed to *al-khaṣṣa* (special people). There was ranking within *al-'āmma* that ranges from shopkeepers and artisans to the very low ranks such as *al-ghawghā'* (mob), *awbāsh al-āmma* (riff-raff), *al-'uyyār* (outlaws) and *al-zu'r* (scoundrels). The greatest cleavage was between the elite and lower orders, but the lower orders themselves were divided on the basis of religion, ethnicity and occupation.

The Ottoman regime did not differ from the Mamluk regime in kind but in degree. The policy of the Ottoman rulers was not to revolutionize the society but rather to control it through the indigenous institutions and groups. During this period few changes took place in the structure of social classes. We find a military elite of Turco-Circassian origin, religious notables, rich merchants, respected men of lower ranks, and the masses. Rebels and slaves occupied the lowest ranks.

Over the years, the power of the Mamluk *amīrs* overruled that of the Ottomans. By the eighteenth century the ruling elite were facing problems of foreign invasion, economic crisis and decline in their power. Increased political instability and a decline of the elite led to some basic changes in the structure of the society. Against the external threats the Mamluks began to seek the support of the indigenous population in order to maintain their privilege and power. For example, the Mamluks began to use Arabic names in this period whereas previously Turkish names were considered necessary for membership in the elite. "Whereas almost all of the Baḥris and Burjis had had Turkish, Mongol or other non-Arab appellations, the Mamluks of the Ottoman period bore Arab names with few exceptions" (Staffa 1977 : 282). It seems that since the elite was blending and intermarrying with some of the indigenous classes of the society, it became difficult for them to maintain a separate identity based on ethnic criteria. Thus we find that the Mamluk elite at the end of the 18th century took on such local titles and labels as *shaykh al-balad* (chief of the town),[2] *al-ummarā'al-*

---

[2] *Shaykh al-balad:* The title *shaykh al-balad* has been noted as having been first applied in the Ottoman archives in the third decade of the eighteenth century to the beylicate of the Mamluks. *Shaykh al-balad* (chief of the town) in that period was a sort of a governor of Egypt, who is the most important bey, chosen by the Dīwān and confirmed by the *pasha*. Some of the Mamluk *Beys* (such as Ali *Bey*) who held that position were so powerful that they acted as independent rulers. Three other terms appear to have been used at this time as synonymous for *shaykh al-balad*. They are *amīr Miṣr*, (Prince of Egypt), *kabīr al-balad* (head of the country), and *kabīr al-qawm* (head of the people). They all indicate a prestigeous label for the highest position among the Mamluk governing body borrowed from the local positions.

miṣrīya (Egyptian princes), *al-agnād al-miṣrīya* (Egyptian soldiers). The ruling elite, which had previously kept itself so aloof, now felt compelled to adopt local expressions of identity.

The structural changes that led to some changes in the elite's identity may have affected the local identity as well. With the decline of the power of the elite there was a relative increase in the economic and political power of lower orders of the society. One may assume that the label *awlād al-balad* emerged at that period as a result of some structural changes in the local society at that period. But to assert such a hypothesis one would require more than the existing scant references dealing with the masses.

1. Awlād al-Balad: Whom to Exclude?

In trying to clarify the connotative meaning attached to *awlād al-balad* and its derivatives[3] particular attention is paid to those contexts where the term *awlād al-balad* was first used in the eighteenth century histographies[4] to distinguish them from other social groups. In this way, their particular characteristics can be delineated.

In the eighteenth century, a Turkish *pasha* acted as the sultan's viceroy. He was installed in the Citadel at the head of a force of Janissaries, 'Azabis, and five other military corps. The offices of the state were held by both Tur-

[3] The derivatives of the epithet *ibn al-balad* as used in the eighteenth century are: *abnā' al-balad, baladī, al-baladiyīn, awlād al-balad, ahl al-balad* and *ahl miṣr*. In philological terms, *ahl al-balad* or *ahl miṣr* is not necessarily a synonym of *awlād al-balad* yet some historians were using these expressions synonymously. See Lane : 27 and al-Jabarti : 633.

[4] Al-Jabartī (1754–1825), the famous Egyptian historian, is the only one who has referred to *awlād al-balad* to any extent in the eighteenth and the beginning of the nineteenth centuries, in his major work *'ajā'ib al-athār fi al-tarājim wal-akhbār*. It was banned until Khedive Tawfiq allowed it to be published in three volumes and nine sections, from 1888 to 1896. It was believed that the censorship was due to al-Jabartī's unflattering references to Muḥammed 'Ali. His work is unique in Arabic historiography. It is more than a history; it is, in the depth and detail of its sociological observations, comparable with the best that has been written in any language. As Ayalon puts it:

> The chronicle is a splendid combination of passionate warmth and scholarly detachment, which is only rarely overcome by any personal or other kind of bias. The reader never loses the feeling of having his finger on the pulse of life and of sharing the true atmosphere of the country and of the period (Ayalon 1960 : 231).

Little escapes his sharp eye – the price of wheat, meat, or butter, the erection of new buildings, public festivals, instruction and civil strife. As effectively as Mayhew (1851–64) caught the spirit of the London poor of the nineteenth century, so does al-Jabartī portray, with unique insight and sympathy, the populace of Cairo during the crowded years of the late eighteenth and early nineteenth centuries.

kish officers and Mamluks. The political power upon which the state rested was vested in the *pasha*, members of the military corps (*ojāqs*), and the *beys*. The *beys* were nominated by the *pasha* to fill important offices. These included the *kākhya* (lieutenant) of the *pasha* who attended the meetings of the *Diwan* as his representative, the four captains of the naval bases, *amīr al-ḥajj* (commander of the pilgrimage), the *defterdār* (register keeper) and the *sanjaq al-khazna* who went with the caravan to Istanbul, *qā'im maqām* (acting viceroy) and five *beys* who acted as governors of important provinces. In theory the power of *ojāq* balanced that of the *beys* but in practice the whole military elite became part of a single Mamluk institution (Staffa 1977 : 278). Struggle for power was continuous among these groups. Though some segments of the ruling elite, such as the Mamluks, were trying to identify with the Egyptians, yet other segments such as soldiers of the *pasha* (who formed the lowest ranks of the military elite) lacked any roots in Egypt. Nevertheless, all segments of the ruling elite were considered foreigners by the indigenous population.

Awlād al-balad were usually indifferent to the ruling elite's internal conflicts. They did not take a stand when the common soldiers revolted against their superiors. For example, when the soldiers were revolting against Muḥammad Pasha (the *wālī*) over their pay in 1803, *awlād al-balad* were asked by the *wālī* to fight the soliders:

> Some of *awlād al-balad* came out of curiosity and passed among the soldiers and no one interfered with them. The soldiers would say: We are separate and you are *ra'īya* (subject people). You can have no relationship with us (al-Jabarti 30 April 1803 : 515).[5]

The *awlād al-balad* were considered by the common soldiers as not only different but also of inferior stock. The ruling class reflected this differentiation in emphasizing their own high position in certain celebrations:

> The blessed Nile reached seventeen Egyptian cubits in height. The barrage was opened on Saturday morning in the presence of the *Pasha*, the *Qādī*, Muhammad 'Alī and the army rank and file. . . . The feast was specially for them, and not for *awlād al-balad* and others (al-Jabartī 18 August 1804 : 604).

The governing elite was a group set apart from *awlād al-balad*; they were also the privileged element within society and *awlād al-balad* the under-

---

[5] References form al-Jabartī are given in the following manner: date of month and year. This is to facilitate locating the exact references since there are many different editions on the market. The edition used here was published by Dar al-Sha'b in Cairo, 1958.

privileged. The governing elite exercised discriminatory prerogatives in regard to them as in the following case:

> It was rumored that Muhammad ‘Alī issued a decree to the *Kāshifs* (governors of districts) of provincial districts, north and south, to buy sheep from the countryside. This was especially for his own consumption as well as for the rations of the soldiers and for people of special status and the people of the state. What was left after that in the slaughter houses fell to the *ahl al-balad* (al-Jarbatī 21 November 1816 : 1972).

Not surprisingly, of all the elite groups it was the soldiers with whom *awlād al-balad* came into the most frequent contact. The soldiers were the coercive arm of government policy and they exploited *awlād al-balad* for their own benefit[6].

Awlād al-balad were also discriminated against under the law, for in practice the legal system was prejudiced against them in favor of other groups. There is reference to the difference before the law in the following:

> It was announced that the *ashrāf*[7] (descendents of the prophet) should be honored and respected and their cases should be presented to *Naqīb* (representative of) *al-ashrāf*. Also the cases of those belonging to the *Abwāb* (military barracks of the Janissary corps) should be presented to their *Ojāq* (military corps) but if someone is from *awlād al-balad*, he has to follow the noble *sharī‘a* (al-Jabartī 11 August 1786 : 151).

The historian Shafiq Ghorbal, commenting on this passage, points out that a thief from *al-ashrāf* could appeal to the *naqib al-ashrāf* and a thief from *al-abwāb* could present his plea to his own *ojāq*, whereas a thief from

---

[6] There are several incidents that indicate the soldiers' exploitation of *awlād al-balad* such as the following:

> Some of the troops used to buy sheep and slaughter them, then sell them at a high price. They would give short weight and *ibn al-balad* could do nothing to check them (al-Jabartī 23 September 1816 : 955).

The exploitation of *awlād al-balad* by the soldiers seems to have been more prevalent in times of crisis. Thus, when a shortage in soap occurred, the *kikhudā* (an officer) fixed its prices and sent a representative to the soap market to supervise sales.

> This representative would only remain for two hours during which only the soldiers crowded in to buy the soap. Later on, the soldiers would sell what they bought, at fixed prices, for a much higher price. Thus *ibn al-balad* was obliged to buy from the soldiers at what ever price they set (al-Jabarti 1816 : 949).

[7] The *ashrāf*, or descendants of the Prophet, from the seventh century onwards occupied a special position of respect in Islamic society. Under their *naqīb*, or leader, they frequently occupied privileged positions under the law and filled responsible posts, although in the eighteenth century many members of the *ashrāf* performed lowly jobs (Levy 1965 : 67) and (Lane 1908 : 135).

awlād al-balad would be liable to have his hand cut off under the terms of Islamic Law. The soldiers were themselves Muslims and yet the *Sharī'a* (Islamic Law) was applied selectively. The Mamluks, according to the Egyptian historian *al-Maqrīzī* (1442), retained their original Mongol law and customs and therefore did not observe the Islamic law in their interpersonal relations. Exceptions were made if the Sultan decided to apply the *Sharī'a* because of a lack or inadequacy in their own laws. Later, the Turks adhered to the same practices as their Mongol predecessors and their refusal to adhere to the *Sharī'a* must have been a significantly alienating factor in the eyes of *awlād al-balad.*

The soldiery disregarded the basic practices of Islam, such as fasting during Ramaḍān:

> *Kitkhudā* (lieutenant) *Bey* and Ayyūb Āgha . . . and the *wālī* patrolled the city stopping in central markets such as al-Ghūrīyya, al-Jamalīyya, Bāb al-Hamzāwi and Bāb Zuwayla and Bāb al-Khalq. Most of their followers were not fasting during Ramaḍān and making a show of it without consideration or respect for this holy month. They would sit in public places and eat and smoke openly without shame. One of them would carelessly blow the smoke into the nose of *ibn al-balad* thus ridiculing the act of fasting (al-Jabartī 24 August 1815 : 922).

This action was all the more comtemptuous, since it was customary in Ramaḍān that no one be seen eating or smoking publicly.

In Cairo at the turn of the nineteenth century, the ruling elite were not the only foreigners; other ethnic groups were also distinct from *awlād al-balad.* The Middle Eastern groups, such as North Africans, Syrians, Sudanese and Yemenis, though Muslims, were identified as distinct from *awlad al-balad* (al-Jabartī: *passim*). These Arab groups shared with *awlād al-balad* a common religion and a common language; some had been resident in Egypt for several generations. However, they were not considered *awlād al-balad* since it was their ancestry and not place of birth which set them apart. Of course, in language and religion there were distinguishing aspects which distinguished them from *awlād al-balad* and underlined the differences inherent in their ethnic backgrounds. First, although they spoke Arabic, North Africans, Syrians and Yemenis spoke dialects that were markedly different from the ordinary Cairene Egyptians. Secondly, they were distinguished by dress.[8] Third, despite their background as Muslims, their educa-

[8] Edward Lane mentions that outward attire was rigidly conformist within various groups and classes of Cairene society. Also foreign travellers (such as Browne and Volney) during this period, as well as scholars of the French Campaign in the *Description de l'Egypte* (Maillet in Tom 3, 9 and 18), have described in detail the type, colour, and style of the different clothing of various groups and classes of the Egyptian society.

tional identities with al-Azhar differed. Frequently, each group had a separate *riwāq* (class) at al-Azhar, such as the Moroccan *riwāq*, and Syrian *riwāq*, etc.

However, more important than dialect, dress or education were the differences in customs, traditions, values and patterns of behavior. We sense in the biographical note about a Tunisian *shaykh* that his assimilation into Egyptian society was, in fact, quite unusual:

> He was born in Tunisia in the year 1152. He was brought up in the Quranic and scholastic tradition. He came to Egypt in the year 1171 and attended al-Azhar University, joining the classes of the North Africans *(riwāq al-Maghāriba)* . . . he mixed with gentle and noble Egyptians and took on their characteristics. He read widely in history and literature and also was talented in relating anecdotes. He married from and adopted the garb and mannerisms of *awlād al-balad* and wrote good poetry (al-Jabartī 22 September 1788 : 201).

The distinguishing characteristics of these individual Middle Eastern groups were enhanced and reinforced by the fact each lived in a separate quarter of Cairo.

Of the groups referred to in the eighteenth century, the Franks (Europeans) constituted the extreme constrast to *awlād al-balad.* They were distinct not only from *awlād al-balad* but also from other Egyptians and Middle Eastern groups as well. The Franks had their separate quarters, as did other ethnic groups. In terms of nationality the Franks in Egypt consisted of six communities,[9] of which the Armenians, Greeks, French and British were the most important. The interaction between the Franks and the indigenous population created a wide range of reaction on the part of the *awlād al-balad,* from wonder at their foreign customs to a sense of technical inadequacy, from a nascent antagonism to a feeling of moral superiority. The local population mistrusted the foreigners and felt no inferiority when comparing themselves with the Franks.

The Franks possessed certain skills completely novel to *awlād al-balad*,

---

The differences were so detailed that they encompassed such items as colour of shoes. For example, the Mamluks wore yellow shoes, the Copts red shoes, the Jews blue shoes, whereas foreigners or Christians were free to wear the Turkish yellow shoes.

[9] This number is based on the estimate of al-Jabarti of consular representatives. He refers to their number in the following passage:

> News arrived of an incident at Alexandria involving Turkish soldiers and different nationalities of Franks . . . . The Franks shot at the soldiers who retaliated by attacking them and fighting them in their own homes. The Franks were in a minority, so the six consuls and their followers went to the shore and wrote a message and sent it to Istanbul and to their own countries (al-Jabarti 17 October 1803 : 546).

such as the use of different kinds of illumination and torches, fireworks and rockets. They also excelled in picturemaking and statues. As foreigners they took interest in visiting antiquities. Their exploration of the exotic, especially old remains, and the money spent on tours, seemed strange to the indigenous population. They tended to specialize in certain professions, particularly those of a scientific nature, such as medicine and engineering. In their work, some of them seemed to show materialistic tendencies which were especially noted by the local population. In a vivid description of those who sought medical treatment from the Franks, al-Jabartī makes his own personal judgement about their ethical values:

> If one of the Frankish doctors was called to cure the rich, he would take money even before leaving his house, assessed according to the rank of the patient. Then he would go to the patient, touch him and pretend to have discovered the cause of his illness. He might exaggerate the case as well as the cure in order to increase his fee. He would insist on taking half the payment for treatment in advance and would continue to charge for each subsequent visit. Also he would make use of their (the Frankish) medicine, which consisted of distilled water from plants, or pommades, and he would make a separate charge for these. This medicine was put in alluring bottles with their (the Frankish) labels ... If God cured the patient he would take the rest of his fees, but if the patient died he would charge his heirs... and if they protested that the patient had died he would reply: I cannot guarantee his life and it is not the doctor's duty to prevent death, or to make life longer (al-Jabartī 8 May 1817 : 978).

The European foreign community in Cairo prior to the nineteenth century was limited in number[10] and power; hence they were a marginal group in the society. By the end of the nineteenth century and especially under Muḥammad 'Alī's rule, the Europeans started to gain importance and were treated, by the ruling elite, differently from the local inhabitants. For example, in cases where medical quacks were exposed, Muslims would have been sentenced to death or to impalement, whereas the European would merely be expelled from the country (al-Jabartī 8 May 1817 : 977). The Franks became not only a privileged group but an influential one so far as the ruling elite was concerned, as the following incident shows:

> When one of the English Franks killed an Albanian, the *fallāḥīn* arrested him and demanded his death from the *kitkhudā*. The *kitk-*

[10] Estimates of the number of Western foreigners in Egypt vary considerably but the important point is that their number started to grow during the rule of Muḥammed 'Alī. By Muḥammed 'Alī's time they became about 10.000 Europeans. But the great influx of Europeans occurred during the time of Sa'īd and Isma'īl. By 1878 their number had risen to 68,653; by 1897 to 112,574, and by 1907 to 151,414 of whom 62,973 were Greek, 34,926 Italian.

> *hudā* refrained from carrying this out because the ruling elite feared the Franks. The *kitkhudā* said: Until we send for the consuls to decide upon the matter we cannot carry out any decision (al-Jabartī 23 January 1820 : 1015).

The Copts were generally differentiated from foreign Christians but in many instances the Christians, including the indigenous Copts, were associated with the foreigners in direct contrast to the Muslims.

> (When the news came that the French had entered Alexandria) the *Amirs* of Egypt (Mamluks) sought out the Frank merchants and imprisoned some of them in the Citadel and some of them in the prince's house. They proceeded to search the houses of the Franks for weapons or other things. Similarly, they searched the houses of the Syrian Christians, the Copts, the Greeks, the churches and the monasteries for weapons. The populace wanted to kill the Christians and Jews but they were prevented by the authorities (al-Jabartī 17 July 1798 : 249).

The Christians were also distinct from *awlād al-balad* in their reaction to the policy of the occupying French who, in their attempt to please the Egyptians, celebrated the traditional feast of the Nile. However, only the ruling elite and Christian communities attended:

> As for *ahl al-balad,* none of them went for an outing in boats that night, as was the custom; only the Syrian Christians, Copts, Turks and the local Franks and their wives did so . . . (al-Jabartī 17 August 1798 : 260).

The association of the indigenous Christians, notably the Copts, with foreign rulers was not a new phenomenon in the history of Egypt. As a minority they were used by rulers in certain occupations such as tax collecting which aroused the local community against them. During the greater part of the period covered by al-Jabartī's chronicle (that is, from 1700 to 1820) their close contact with foreign elements and their identification with them is a recurring theme in the literature. For example, when the French wanted to exploit the country by imposing more taxes and controlling its resources they made use of Copts who were described as follows:

> The Copts were sent to villages as *kāshifs* with the French soldiers. They would demand forcibly impossible sums of money from the villagers. If they did not supply the money in a few hours, they would be subjected to all sorts of tyranny such as beating and dragging behind horses. If they ran away the village would be plundered and then burned. To please the French the Copts exceeded them in their terrorism (al-Jabarti 15 May 1800 : 272).

This collaboration of some Copts with the French gave them certain economic privileges that they were not able to attain before:

> The increase in taxation in the provinces was due to the advice of the Copts because they were the ones who occupied high posts in the

> state. They committed themselves to the French to collect taxes. They divided the provinces among themselves. Each one of them acted as a great prince. He lived lavishly in the center of the province surrounded by the French soldiers, clerks, clients, servants, cooks, etc. (al-Jabartī 15 May 1800 : 371).

The utilization of the Copts by the French was continued by Muḥammad 'Alī who was mainly concerned with collecting money by any means in order to carry out his schemes of modernization. Those who agreed with his policy became his close attendants; those who tried to advise otherwise or contradict him such as some of the notables, were dismissed and disgraced. His entourage is described as consisting mainly of Christians who are depicted in the literature as submitting to Muḥammad 'Alī's scheme to maintain power primarily through exploiting the Muslim masses.

> The Christians were consulted in all important decisions. They tried to please Muḥammad 'Alī and carry out his projects, improve his plans (of monopolization) or draw his attention to possibilities he had overlooked in improving his schemes of getting to the profits and income of craftsmen, thus taking even what they had kept for their living (al-Jabartī 21 November 1816 : 971).

Therefore their distinct religion and occupations, in addition to the role they played within the foreign community, gave them a negative image among the Muslim indigenous population.

2. Awlād al-Balad: Whom to Include?

The label *awlād al-balad* has thus far been used to analyze indigenous groups vis-a-vis groups who possess certain foreign elements. However, within the indigenous group itself *awlād al-balad* represents a certain subsection, in which the *fallāḥīn*, for example, were clearly not included:

> The *kāshif* responsible for Bāb al-Futūḥ used to take money from those who passed by. If the passer-by was dressed as a *fallāḥ*, that is, wearing a *jubba* (a long outer garment of wool) or a *za'but*, the *kāshif* took all he had, or ten *niṣf* if he was poor. But if he was from *awlād al-balad* and of good appearance, or dressed in *jūkha*, (an overcoat only worn by the rich) even if it were old, he was requested to pay a thousand *niṣf* or else he was imprisoned (al-Jabartī January 1804 : 553).

This incident explicitly refers to the distinction between *awlād al-balad* and the *fallāḥīn*. A difference in dress reflects the superior economic status of *awlād al-balad*, to judge from the sums of money demanded from each group. Economic status, however, is not the only factor that sets off *awlād al-balad* from the *fallāḥīn. Awlād al-balad*, (while possibly of distant rural origin), are urbanites, born and bred in cities, and are employed in urban vocations. This is implied in the defence made by *awlād al-balad* who were caught by Muḥammad 'Alī's clients in respect of the land tax they had to pay.

> They (the *rūznāmijī* or director of the scribes of the Treasury and soldiers) were pursuing *awlād al-balad* and those who had old connections with the villages. A person (*ibn al-balad)* would be sitting in his shop and suddenly would find himself surrounded by soldiers and dragged to Muḥammad 'Alī's assistants without knowing his offence. He would ask: 'What is my offence?' They would answer him: 'You have to pay your land tax.' He would say 'What land tax?' They would answer: 'The taxes you have not paid in return for cultivation of your land for years.' It amounts to such and such. *Ibn al-balad* would say: 'But I do not know about this. Neither I, nor my father, nor my grandfather knew the *balad,* nor have I seen it all my life'. They would tell him 'Are you so and so the *Mīnyāwī* or *Shubrawī*,[11] i.e. from the village Shubra or Minya?' He would answer: 'This is an old connection which came to me from my uncle or my grandfather'. This was no excuse and he would be beaten and imprisoned . . . this happened to many shopkeepers, merchants and silk craftsmen (al-Jabartī 27 August 1808 : 757).

The term *awlād al-balad,* however, does not apply to just any indigenous urbanite community. It was specifically used when referring to the Cairene indigenous Muslim community, hence phrases such as *ahl al-balad* and *ahl miṣr* were used interchangeably. Moreover, it appears that *awlād al-balad* were indigenous Muslim Cairenes. This implicit connotation of the term *awlād al-balad* in the eighteenth century was referred to explicitly in the the nineteenth century by Edward Lane.

> The native Muslim inhabitants of Cairo commonly call themselves *"El-Masreyeen", "Awlād Masr"* (or *"Ahl Masr"*) and *"Awlād el-Beled",* which signify People of Masr, Children of Masr, and Children of the Town: the singular forms of these appellations are "Masree", "Ibn Masr", and "Ibn el-Beled". Of these three terms, the last is most common in the town itself (Lane 1908 : 27).

The question must now be raised as to whether the label *awlād al-balad* was indicative of *all* indigenous Cairenes. In the following pages, I propose to explore the degree to which the concept of *awlād al-balad* was identifiable with the indigenous categorization which existed at that time.

---

[11] A person's last name, when derived from that of a village or a town, is an indication that the person originates from that place.

The main indigenous Cairene categorizations which major Arabic histographies of that period enumerate are: *al-'ulamā'* (religious scholars) and *al-tujjār* (merchants). Second to the group of *'ulamā'* and merchants are the common people, i.e. *al-'āmma* or *ra'īyya* (subject masses). They were generally the working and trading people of the city such as *arbāb al-sanā'ī'* (craftsmen) and *al-sūqa* (food retailers and shopkeepers). A lower group of *al-'āmma* who are identified as the *ardhāl al-'āmma* (lowest of the common people), *awbāsh al-'āmma* (riff-raff of the common people) and *ghawghā'* (trouble-makers). The lowest groups are associated with disreputable works (on religious grounds) such as usurers, brokers, slave dealers, etc. People of questionable morality such as prostitutes, wine sellers, dancers and entertainers are also from the lowest groups. Other menial groups are those who work as kitchen boys, servants, gatekeepers, waterboys of the bath, donkey drivers, dog handlers, irregularly employed people and beggars. Other groups that are associated with the city mob are the *zu'r* (scoundrels), the *shuṭṭār* (the clever), and the *'uṣab* (bands). These groups are associated with criminal acts and violence in the city.

Of the previously mentioned groups the *'ulamā'* occupied the highest status in the social stratification of the indigenous population because of their religious power. The fact that all aspects of life (social, economic and political) were governed by the religious laws encouraged a strong tie between the *'ulamā'* and the ruling elite. The foreign ruling elite needed the religious backing of the *'ulamā'*. The political power of the *'ulamā'* was asserted by the role they played as middlemen between the people and the ruling elite.

During the last decade of the eighteenth century the power of the Mamluk *beys* was waning and the *'ulamā'* came to the fore as popular leaders. With the coming of Napoleon and the disintegration of the military elite, the *'ulamā'* played an important role in filling the political vacuum that began to appear. As a European power, the French were incapable of governing without their help. Napoleon set up councils composed of leading religious and commercial notables. The General Council debated serious issues of national interest, from laws of inheritance and criminal justice to taxation (Staffa 1977 : 298).

While some *'ulamā'* cooperated for a while with the French, very soon resistance appeared. The *'ulamā'* animated the populace against the French and they led a series of popular revolts which resulted in the withdrawal of the French. In that period the country was faced with economic and political chaos and the *'ulamā'* came to the fore and played a significant role in the rise of Muḥammād 'Alī to power. Thus the power of the *'ulamā'* increased tremendously in the last few decades of Mamluk rule up to Muḥammad 'Alī's accession to power.

> By the eighteenth century when the coercive power (of rulers) had become weak or diffused and when long established customs had given them a practical immunity from arbitrary execution and punishment, they *('ulamā')* could afford to brave the displeasure of *Pashas* and *Beys* and they were able to oppose rulers with some measure of success and even able to lead movements of opposition (Loutfi el-Sayed 1968 : 265).

Part of the strength of the *'ulamā'* by the end of the eighteenth century was due to their economic status. Some *'ulamā'* were exceptionally wealthy, and were among the chief *multazims* in Egypt. Since the introduction of the *iltizām*[12] ; system in the mid-sixteenth century, there were *'ulamā' multazims*, but they constituted only a minor group compared to the Mamluk elite or soldiery. But by the end of the eighteenth century the number of *'ulamā' multazims* had reached 307, thus composing seven percent of all *multazims* in Egypt (Abd al-Rahim 1974 : 88). Some *'ulamā'* became *multazims* of several villages which included their own original homes, thus adding to their power and prestige. Like the Mamluk princes, many of the *'ulamā'* in this category built luxurious palaces and took enormous interest in their property and wealth.

The most powerful of the *'ulamā'* were those who occupied official positions in the religious hierarchy such as, first, the Rector of al-Azhar, the *muftīs* and the *naqīb al-ashrāf* (marshal of the notables), and next the heads of the two most popular sufi orders. These two *Shaykhs* were so powerful at the time that "they had the ability to assemble in a single day a powerful military regiment of at least seventy or eighty thousand men who are docile and loyal to them" (Shaw 1962 : 22–23).

It was the religious leaders of the sufi orders, however, who played the most effective political role, since they were capable of maintaining economic and political independence. Membership in these orders cut across every level of the society. In addition, membership in sufi order coincided with membership in certain occupational guilds. This firm connection gave certain sufi orders control over the economic sector.

---

[12] *Iltizām* was a system of farm-tax which was not directly controlled by government. It was carried by individual Mamluk princes, military personnel, *shaykhs* of Bedouins, *'ulamā'*, merchants, or whoever expressed the wish to collect the taxes assigned on lands of a certain village or villages for a specific time. *Iltizām* was given in an auction and whoever took it was obliged to pay the tax to the government; after getting a certain contract he would become a *multazim*. He was then entitled to raise whatever monies he could from the peasants. At the beginning, *iltizām* was only for a few years but later, in the eighteenth century, the right to inherit *iltizāms* became common. The new procedure solidified the position of certain *multazims* in the area in which they possessed *iltizām* to the extent that some villages were identified by their *multazims* ('Abd al-Raḥīm 1974 :67–99).

In spite of the fact that a faction of the religious notables at certain times formed part of the aristocratic elite, frequently working in conjunction with the Ottomans and Mamluks and enjoying special privileges, we believe that the *'ulamā'* as a whole were considered *awlād al-balad.* They were closely linked with the masses at all levels.[13] The masses looked to the *'ulamā'* for advice, representation and leadership. The informal relationship between the *'ulamā'* and the common people was institutionalized in many instances for political purposes. There are numerous episodes in the chronicles of the eighteenth century that reveal the solidarity of the *'ulamā'* with the common people against the Mamluk princes as, for example, the significant incident in Sharqīya (the province in which the influential scholar, Shaykh al-Sharqāwī had land). In 1795, the people of Sharqīya complained to Shaykh al-Sharqāwī of the injustice of Muḥammad Bey al-'Alfī (an influential Mamluk) in imposing new taxes. Shaykh al-Sharqāwī became angry, gathered other *Shaykhs* at al-Azhar and closed its doors to indicate a strike was on. The *'ulamā'* also ordered the people to close the shops and markets and to start a big demonstration. When the Mamluk governor attempted to find out what their demands were they said, "We want justice, release from tyranny, the application of the *Sharī'a* and the cancelling of newly created taxations". The *defterdār* (register keeper) answered: "We cannot abide by all your demands because this will affect our livelihood and expenses." The *'ulamā'* answered back: "This is no excuse. Why all this expenditure and purchasing of slaves? After all, a prince is considered a prince only by what he gives and not by what he takes." The strike and demonstrations of the masses went on for days while the *'ulamā',* the Mamluk princes and the governor negotiated. Finally, the issue was resolved when "the Mamluk princes were forced to submit to the *'ulamā'*. They confessed their guilt and vowed that they would never levy high taxes". Solidarity between the *'ulama'* and the masses against the Mamluk princes ended with a guarantee from the Mamluk princes that they themselves would levy all new taxation, would restrain their clients from exploiting the people, and would abide by their customary obligations of serving the people. The *Shaykhs* went back to their residences surrounded by the common people *(al-'āmma)* who were calling: "as our masters the *'ulamā'* planned it all; now tyranny, taxation and injustice have ended throughout Egyptian lands" (al-Jabartī June 1795).

---

[13] An important link between the *'ulamā'* and the masses was through guilds and Sufi orders. Guilds were often set within the mosque precincts. Even the apprentice certificates were religiously phrased and *'ulamā'* and *shaykhs* of corporations often aided and conferred with each other. In fact, al-Jabartī's father corrected weights and measures and did fine marble inlay himself. Guild members and *'ulamā'* were frequently members of the Sufi orders, al-Azhar being the center of Sufism in the sixteenth century (Holt 1968 : 266).

The symbiotic relation between the *'ulamā'* and the masses worked two ways: one way was that if the *'ulamā'* objected to government measures they would arouse the populace against them. The other direction was that when a group of *al-āmma*, a quarter, or even an individual had been mistreated, complaints would be made to the *'ulamā'*. In certain cases some *'ulamā'* were less than enthusiastic in taking action against the ruling elite. Hence the populace would force them to act as in the case of *Shaykh* al-'Arūsī in 1787 when a group of merchants and shopkeepers complained of an extra tax that Ismā'īl *Bey* tried to levy. They gathered in Al-Azhar and shut its doors. *Shaykh* al-'Arusi tried to prevent them. The merchants and shopkeepers, accompanied by the populace, were cursing the *'ulamā'* until *Shaykh* al-'Arūsī was forced to go to the *wālī* who forwarded the complaints to Ismā'īl *Bey*. Ismā'īl *Bey* was furious and thought that *Shaykh* al-'Arūsī was the one who aroused the masses. But the messengers swore that he was innocent of that charge and that his intention, i.e. submitting to the masses, was to get rid of them (al-Jabartī 27 October 1787 : 184). Similar incidents indicate that the *'ulamā,* even when they wanted to submit to the elite, were forced by the people to collaborate and defend their cause. The collaboration between the masses and the *'ulamā'* had reached its peak in the revolt against the Turkish ruler Taher Pasha, causing his downfall and the accession of Muḥammad 'Alī in 1805. Their sense of solidarity and identity as *ahl al-balad* was expressed as follows:

> Those in authority are the *'ulamā'* and the followers of the *Sharī'a* and the righteous Sultan, but this is a tyrannical man (Tāher Pasha) and it is the tradition from time immemorial that *ahl al-balad* depose the wālī if he be unjust (al-Jabartī 25 May 1805 : 630).

The *'ulamā'* were therefore frequently identified with the masses, and constituted the leadership element amongst them. We can deduce from the previous survey that the masses looked upon the *'ulamā'* as guardians of religion and interpreters of the *Sharī'a*, thus accepting their leadership. Hence their identification as *awlād al-balad* seems to be necessary.

The second notable group of the Cairene society comprised the rich merchants whose power was based on their access to economic resources. Before the economic decline of the sixteenth, seventeenth and eighteenth centuries, the wealth of some merchants rivalled that of the ruling elite. Their social power was solidified with the formal and informal ties they had with the elite. This liaison had positive and negative effects upon merchants:

> "when affluent, the elite invested thousands of dinars in commercial expeditions, but when they needed ready cash, either for defense against an external threat or to meet internal challenges to their power, it was to the merchants that they turned. All too often the sale

of excess supplies became an extortionate forced purchase (ṭarḥ) and heavy loans demanded by the rulers were scantily repaid or not repaid at all" (Staffa 1977 : 173).

Even in the eighteenth century when commercial activity was shrinking, many merchants continued to serve as sources of wealth and prestige. One of these merchants was described as follows:

> He was one of the notable and famous merchants, as were his ancestors. His well-known residence at Azbakīya is the house of honor, fame and pride. His Mamluks were from the Egyptian notables (al-Jabartī March 1757 : 70).

Not only did some merchants achieve a high status in society but, as a whole, merchants were respected and their guilds ranked highest amongst all other guilds. The high respect for their position was associated in guild lore with the Prophet Muḥammad, who was a merchant. Merchant guilds and corporations in Cairo in the eighteenth century were highly organized and relatively independent of the central authority. Within the organization of merchants there was a hierarchy of ranks in which import-export merchants were the highest. These were the merchants who were closely allied with the ruling elite. The artisans and small merchants were economically and politically less important. At the top of the organization was the *Shāh Bandar,* or Chief Representative of the Merchants whose role was an important one extending far beyond the internal organization of the merchant guilds. This is illustrated in the biography of one such chief representative al-Sayyid Muḥammad al-Maḥrūqī:

> He was in charge of all the business concerning travel and caravans, all messages received and sent to Hijāz, all taxes levied upon ship and caravan loads, and all the various aspects of import and export. He was also responsible for all the different tribes; their disputes, their policies and their legal councils. He was also in charge of arbitration in cases concerning merchants, vendors, and local artisans. He was responsible for the Pasha's missions, correspondence, trade, commercial ventures, taxes, and the giving of instructions to soldiers (in the Hijāz) for the campaigning against the Wahhābīs (al-Jabartī 21 November 1816 : 970).

It is interesting to observe that al-Maḥrūqī, *Shāh Bandar* of Merchants, for all his influence and wealth, was clearly identified with *awlād al-balad:*

> His orders were carried out in Egypt, Turkey, the Hijāz and Syria, and he achieved fame and power as no one else before him from among *awlād al-balad* (al-Jabartī 29 March 1805 : 623).

However, this identity was not unique to al-Maḥrūqī alone but extended to all merchants and artisans: "A tax was levied on the *ahl al-balad* apportioned among artisans and merchants" (al-Jabartī 29 March 1805 : 623). The artisans, although of a lower status and different occupation than merchants, were usually associated with them and were highly respected. Lane did not hesitate to class artisans with merchants of all kinds (Staffa 1877 : 137).

In order to protect their commercial and economic interests, merchants' cooperation with the military elite was essential. This cooperation could have led naturally to a closer identification between them were it not for the fact that the ruling elite were foreigners and that they never fully allowed indigenous sectors to be part of them however wealthy they were. At the same time, the rich merchants retained the indigenous identity as members of guilds in which they had to cooperate with the various ranks of merchants to face the common misfortunes of trade which could come about through natural or political causes.

The merchants' power, as that of the *'ulamā'*, was increasing while that of the ruling elite was declining. The merchants were able to avoid government interference. Their increasing feeling of superiority and importance as well as an intransigent attitude toward authority is well illustrated in their relations to the Turkish governors:

> The Beduins robbed the caravan of some Cairene merchants. So the latter went complaining to the *wālī*, who told them that they deserved it because they tricked him by escaping taxation. Sayyid Bakir answered him saying: 'My lord Minister, it has been customary for merchants to do this and justify it but it is up to the governor to investigate and examine it.' The minister was outraged by this answer and said: 'Look at how he answers, discusses, and throws back words and arguments. Never have I seen such people and impoliteness as that of these *ahl al-balad'*. And his hands started trembling with anger (al-Jabarti 8 July 1788 : 197).

Thus, although merchants would be easily identified with the ruling elite, they were nevertheless labelled as *awlād al-balad.* It seems that to assert their power and to protect their interest, the merchants needed the support of the indigenous population, especially when the elitest power began to shrink such that their protection was no longer as effective as before.

So far, we have been dealing with three groups (*'ulamā'*, merchants and artisans), who, by virtue of their economic and religious positions, had acquired a high rank in the Cairene social structure and yet were identified as *awlād al-balad.* The rest of the Cairene groups were of a lower status and their labels *(awbāsh, sūqa, zu'r, ghawghā', al-harāfīsh)* had a pejorative meaning. Would these groups have been considered *awlād al-balad?*

At the end of the eigtheenth century there are indications that low status groups were exluded from the term *awlād al-balad.* At that time, guilds of low rank (*al-ḥiraf al-dunya*) included sellers of pastries, fryers of fish, cooks, the donkey drivers, etc. and of still lower rank were guilds whose members were engaged in criminal or immoral jobs, irregular work and menial tasks. Members of these low status jobs were mainly recruited from migrant peasants and Nubians and were referred to as distinct from *awlād al-balad* in such references as: "The soldiers started stealing the donkeys of *awlād al-balad.* They stole the donkeys of the water carriers who delivered the water from the *Khalīj.*" (al-Jabartī : 496). Hence, *awlād al-balad* were usually associated with higher status jobs and it was only in times of economic crisis that their status might degenerate so that they would be forced to resort to other more menial jobs:

> Many of *arbāb al-ṣanā'i'* (craftsman) whose crafts did not have markets had to earn their living by 'low crafts' (*al-hiraf al-dunya*) such as frying fish, selling pastries, cooking, opening coffee shops. As for those who were occupied in low-rank crafts most of them worked as donkey-drivers (al-Jabartī February 1799 : 294).

Although the lowest status groups were excluded from the category of *awlād al-balad* on economic, ethnic and rural bases, one could argue that these same low income groups would be identified as *awlād al-balad* on the basis of residence. They were co-dwellers in the popular quarters with the high status groups, and the inhabitants of these quarters were labelled as *awlād al-balad.* The organization of the Cairene quarters and their role in the popular revolts of the eighteenth and nineteenth centuries seem to have integrated the different economic strata of the indigenous population into the cohesive identity of *awlād al-balad*. The city of Cairo was divided into subsections called *ḥārāt* or quarters. These *ḥārāt* formed a homogeneous unit. The solidarity of some *ḥārāt* was based on religious, ethnic, racial or occupational identity. Each *ḥāra* was physically barricaded from other *ḥārāt* by walls and gates that were closed at night and in time of crisis. It was guarded by the *bawwābs* (doorkeepers) whose duty was to lock the doors at night. Politically the *ḥāra* was a unit of administration and control (Abu-Lughod 1970 : 24). Each *ḥāra* had its own *shaykh*, who was called *shaykh al-ḥāra* and whose function was to maintain order, to settle disputes among the inhabitants, and to expel those who disturbed the peace of the quarter.

The only general information we have of the informal structure of these popular quarters is in times of crisis and revolt. Very little is known about their internal network of relations. Scattered evidence indicates that there were close ties within the same *ḥāra* as well as among popular *ḥārāt* and that various strata of the dwellers of these *ḥārāt* were organized and unified in institutionalized religious orders and occupational structures (guilds) as well as around the informal leaders of these *ḥārāt.* The unified identity of the *ḥāra* could also be seen during public ceremonies such as weddings, funerals and birthdays (*mawlids*) of saints. Another element which brought about an *esprit de corps* in the quarter was the role played by the youth.

The youth of each *ḥāra* formed gangs that were labelled by various names such as *'usab, zu'ar* and *shuṭṭār,* who performed the role of protection and were sensitive to the identity of their *ḥāra* vis-a-vis other *ḥārāt*. Since different quarters or *ḥārāt* were occupied by different groups whose interests were different, conflict between them might be expected. It seems possible that the *zu'ar, 'usab* and *shuṭṭār* played the role of informal leadership which in the beginning of the twentieth century, was performed by the *futūwa*. (See chapter III for the details of the role of the *futūwa*).

Though we cannot divide Cairene quarters on a basis of class, there were certain aristocratic quarters that were favored by the elite and the wealthy. On the other hand, there were popular quarters that had a concentration of indigenous Muslims, i.e. *awlād al-balad.* The popular quarters were the communities of *'ulamā'*, merchants, artisans, and low status groups of *al-'āmma;* that is, the rich and poor segments of *awlād al-balad* together. But there were also sub-categorizations of popular quarters according to certain occupations and Muslim religious orders. For example, Ḥusaynīyya had a concentration of butchers and members of the Bayūmīyya Sufi order. In the eighteenth century the butchers were exceedingly numerous, having three corporations with a total of 2,200 members. The quarter was one of the most effectively organized in town. Under Ahmed Salim al-Jazzār the butcher, the *shaykh* of the Bayūmīyya, the quarter rebelled twice against the impositions of Murad-Bey in 1786 and 1790 (Staffa 1977 : 269). There was a strong association between this Sufi order, the butchers' guild and the quarter. The leader of Bayūmīyya, 'Alī al-Bayūmī, lived in the quarter and his tomb and mosque in the quarter became the center of religious activity of the order. In another popular quarter, Bab al-Sha'riyya, the dominant occupation was that of grain merchant. Al-Rumayla was another popular quarter in which the principle activity of the population was grain and vegetable trading. In general, popular quarters were associated with industries that dealt with food products and the preparation of raw materials, slaughtering of animals, pressing of oil, tanning of skin and the preparation and distribution of grains, legumes, and fruits (Staffa 1977 : 259). Dwellers of these popular quarters were labeled by the term *awlād al-balad.*

Solidarity of these quarters was reinforced by a common rebellious attitude toward the ruling elite. The people of these quarters, i.e. *awlād al-balad,* were certainly not submissive in their reaction to authority. Their attitude is reflected in the numerous clashes they had with the ruling body as the following incidents indicate:

> On Saturday, the eighth, a fight broke out between *ahl Būlāq* and the soldiers because of their (soldiers) corruption and seduction of women. Also because of the trouble they caused to the commoners (*sūqā*) and shopowners and their robbing of goods. A group of the people of Būlāq gathered outside the town to go to the Pasha to complain about

> the misery that had befallen them. Upon hearing this the armed soldiers of Qualyūnjīya attacked them. The Qalyūnjīya were defeated, upon which the 'Agha appeared and settled the matter by pacifying the commoners (al-Jabartī 15 February 1788 : 190).
>
> A clash occurred between the soldiers and *ahl al-balad* at Bāb al-Sha'rīyya over housing and similarly at Bāb al-Lūq, Būlāq and Old Cairo and many were killed (al-Jabartī 11 July 1805 : 637).
>
> While one of the *awlād al-balad* was going in the direction of al-Khurūn-fish, he was attacked and killed by some *'Hagu'* soldiers living in the house of Shāhīn Kāshif. The people of the district rose in revolt and shots were exchanged (al-Jabartī 11 July 1805 : 637).
>
> If something occurred between the inhabitants of the Rumayla quarter and the soldiers, those in the Citadel would rejoice and incite *awlād al-balad* against them. Amongst them also (i.e. the garrison in the Citadel) were those who incited the troops against *awlād al-balad* and said to them, in their own tongue and also in Arabic: 'Beat the *fallāhīn'* (al-Jabartī 9 June 1805 : 633).

Awlād al-balad appear to have been infused not only by a spirit of rebelliousness but also by a capacity and spirit to ridicule and mock the ruling elite as the following excerpt indicates:

> Salīm 'Āgha called on a party of Qalyūnjīya and Arna'ūd and the Syrians to leave without delay. Whoever would be found after three days would deserve what befell him. The Mamluks went about humiliating and disarming whoever they met of them. Some of them met together and went to the Pasha and he sent with them one of the *dulāt* (soldiers) who took them down to Būlāq in boats. *Awlād al-balad* and the children went about ridiculing and whistling at them all along the way (al-Jabartī 23 July 1791 : 222).

Lane referred to this tendency of ridiculing and mocking the ruling elite as follows: "The Egyptians are particularly prone to satire and often display considerable wit in their jeers and jests. Their language affords them great facilities for punning and for ambiguous conversation, in which they very frequently indulge. The lower orders sometimes lampoon their rulers in songs and ridicule those enactments of the government by which they themselves suffer.... A Song ... which was composed on the occasion of an increase of the income-tax called (*firdeh*) began thus: You who have (nothing on your head but) a *libdeh* (head cover of the poor) sell it and pay the *firdeh*" (Lane 1908 : 314).

The rebellious spirit of *awlād al-balad* was not limited to minor, individual clashes but extended to rebellious actions that embraced all the popular quarters and Cairene masses. The internal structure of the quarters seems to have facilitated the mobilization of various segments of *awlād al-balad.* In these quarters it seems that the groups identified as *zu'r, shuṭṭār, 'uyyāq* and *'uṣab* (see Introd. p. 4, n. 5) acted as informal leaders with the support of the people, and that they were able to extend their protection to various indigenous segments of the society against foreign elites. For example, Shaykh al-Kafrāwī, one of the *'ūlamā'*, opposed the Mamluk elite on various occasions, but he could not be harmed because "he was married to the daughter of *mu'allim Dar'ā,* the butcher of Ḥusayniyya; thus he got the protection of the people of the quarter, *al-zu'r* and *al-shuṭṭār*" (al-Jabartī 22 September 1788 : 200). It seems that these groups by themselves were so reputed for their strength and boldness that they intimidated certain groups of the ruling elite. The collaboration of the various leaders of the different segments (*'ulamā'* and masses) of *awlād al-balad* was effective in stopping many of the unjust measures that were ordered, such as the imposition of taxes, the arrest of people or the plundering of towns or quarters. In one instance of plundering, for example, the *zu'r* rallied the people of the Husayniyya quarter led by Shaykh al-Dardiri threatening to plunder the house of the ruling elite. Fearing the consequences, the Mamluks promised the mob that they would return all the spoils and that a sort of jury would be appointed to investigate the perpetrators of the abuse. One of the latter, when reproached for his deeds by the Mamluk Governor, declared: "We are all plunderers–you, Ibrāhīm Bey (the Governor) plunder, Murād Bey (another Governor) plunders, and I plunder too" (al-Jabartī 3 March 1786: 136).

When the ruling elite was foreign and non-Muslim the revolt of the *awlād al-balad* was intensified because it became a religious cause as well as a national one. Resistance to the French took the form of two major popular uprisings in 1798 and 1800. In view of the new weaponry that the French employed in Egypt and the ignorance of the masses of their fire power, one can appreciate the bravery of the people of Husaynīyya in confronting Napoleon's troops:

> . . . Many of the *ghawghā* (mob) united and proclaimed *al-Jihād* (holy war) and brought their hidden weapons of war and resistance . . . they were joined by *ḥasharāt al-Ḥusaynīyya* (insects of al-Husaynīyya) and the *zu'r al-ḥārāt of Baranīyya*. They were shouting "God save Islam". They proceeded to the house of judges and were followed by another thousand or more like them (denoting *zu'r*) . . . when the French knew of their gathering a French leader with his troops proceeded to their popular quarters but the *zu'r* were fortified behind barricades and they killed several soldiers and prevented them from entering their quarters . . . The French shelled the quarters that surrounded al-Azhar and directed their fire at the mosque of al-Azhar. The people of the quarters were alarmed and ran away since they had not seen such missiles before. As for the people of al-Husaynīyya and al-'Atuf, they went on fighting until their gun powder was exhausted while the French fired constantly. Finally, having exhausted their arms and unable to continue, they left their position to the French (al-Jabartī 21 October 1798 : 273–5).

Such incidents indicate the role of *awlād al-balad* and the unity they achieved in political crisis. They were armed, although not at the same level as the French, but still effective in resistance. Their leadership of the quarters in collaboration with the religious leaders was most effective. The most important example of the efficiency of the collaboration among the *'ulamā'*, the masses of the people of the popular quarters, and their informal leaders, was seen in the revolt against the Turkish ruler of Egypt (Tāher Pasha), causing his downfall and leading to the accession of Muḥammad 'Alī (1805). This seems to have been the last effective revolt in which this coalition confronted the ruling elite.

Thus we can say that the specific collectivity identified as *awlād al-balad* in the eighteenth century and the beginning of the nineteenth century consisted of the *'ulamā'*, merchants and artisans, and the Cairene masses.

3. Who Were Awlād al-Balad at the Beginning of the Twentieth Century?

The transformation of the Egyptian economy during the nineteenth century, resulting from both Muḥammad 'Alī's measures and later the British occupation, and the accompanying social changes, altered the existing map of social relations as well as the status of the social groups in Cairene society.

Within the foreign sphere certain ethnic groups disappeared while others came to the forefront. By the beginning of the twentieth century an ethnically, racially or religiously separate Middle Eastern community such as in the eighteenth century is rarely heard of. With the rise of a national consciousness these groups became assimilated in the country as Egyptians. The Turco-Circassian group in particular, which used to occupy the elite status in Cairene society was slowly dissolving. During the eighteenth century, senior posts in the government and the army had been held by a Turkish-speaking minority, the descendents of Mamluk slaves or of officials sent from Istanbul. Later, during the early nineteenth century many of them were replaced by Ottoman soldiers of fortune who had served in Muḥammad 'Alī's army. In the course of time their importance as a separate group began to diminish once the administration became more Egyptianized. Meanwhile, for their part, more of the Turco-Circassians married Egyptian women and thus became assimilated.

While the foreign Turco-Circassian group was deteriorating as an elite, their political control being slowly dismantled, another foreign group, the European, was taking over. The number of Europeans in Egypt rose from approximately 8,000–10,000 in 1838 to over 90,000 in 1881 and 151,414 in 1907 (Owen 1972). The majority of the foreign community was engaged in banking and finance. These foreigners occupied a privileged position as a result of the Capitulation Laws, the treaties governing the status of foreigners within the Ottoman Empire. By the end of the nineteenth century their power was crowned by military occupation and complete control over the country. The rise of the European community to an elitist rank within the Egyptian society accelerated the spread of Western culture. The European community in Egypt in the twentieth century became an aristocratic, privileged group which exploited the Egyptians and enjoyed a luxurious life. An Egyptian novelist[14] critically recorded the changes occurring in Egyptian society during the late nineteenth and early twentieth centuries. We read, for example, of an exchange between a *pasha* and a lawyer.

Pasha: Would you inform me about the location of this Paradise in Cairo?

Lawyer: This is the Isma'īlīya quarter established by Isma'īl to beautify the Nile Valley. A group of wealthy aristocrats reside there.

Pasha: Great for the Egyptians! Finally destiny has smiled upon them and changed their misery to fortune and housed them in these marvellous palaces instead of ruins.

Lawyer: Dear prince, don't envy the Egyptian for this fortune; come and lament with me his misfortune. He doesn't possess one house to settle in in this "paradise". Everything you see belongs to the foreigners.

Pasha: How come the foreigners instead of the natives possess this paradise and take hold of these palaces?

Lawyer: The Egyptians have brought on their own fate. They changed (their) fortune to misfortune . . . Consequently this is the fate of those who throw themselves open to foreigners; those who help a tyrant fall prey to his tyranny (al-Muwaylihī 1903 : 46–47).

[14] Al-Muwaylihi (1858–1930) a student of Gamal al-Din al-Afghani and Muhammed 'Abdou. His book *Ḥadīth 'Īsā ibn Hishām* is one of the first attempts of Egyptian novels. Thus he combines in this book both the techniques of the old Arabic *maqāmāt* (short stories narrated by an imaginary figure) and that of the European novel. As a literary endeavor, it is considered naive in its character development and plot. However, it is a unique literary source for social conditions in the dynamic years that preceded the 1919 Revolution. The plot revolves around a dialogue between an imaginary *Pasha* from the time of Muḥammed 'Alī who is resurrected from his grave, and the author, disguised as 'Īsa ibn Hishām, a writer in the 1900's. The novel is principally a record of conditions prevailing in various strata in the Egyptian society. He succeeded in projecting the confusion, unrest and pessimism that prevailed among all strata in this period. As a writer and intellectual, his critical view and negative orientation toward changes that were taking place at that time (mainly westernization) reflect a common trend among intellectuals of that period.

The European community in Egypt in the twentieth century, instead of being marginal and isolated groups as in the eighteenth and nineteenth centuries, became influential and elitist looking down on the Egyptians and treating them as second class citizens. This social process of transformation of the elitist status from one foreign group to another is described perceptively in a statement by an Egyptian lawyer to the Turkish *Pasha* as follows:

> As if fate has granted the Mamluks dominance over the Egyptians so as to plunder their wealth and steal their sustenance. Then fate gave you (Turks) supremacy over them (Mamluks) to plunder what they had amassed. Then fate gave dominance to your descendents who submitted everything to the foreigner. The latter delighted in extravagance in front of the Egyptian who was in desperate need of even the smallest part of it. And what forced your descendents into that passivity and submission is the respect for foreigners and disdain for Egyptians which they have inherited from you. It did not suffice you to be sovereigns of the Egyptians but then you granted foreigners partnership in this sovereignty. The foreigners in turn, usurped the sovereignty and submitted you, together with the Egyptians, to slavery. Thus masters and slaves became one (al-Muwaylihī 1903 : 54).

In this statement and others similar to it, the Egyptian novelist, al-Muwaylihī, is hinting at the internal factors that led to the downfall of the Turkish elite. He refers mainly to the tyranny and unjust measures of this group and their deviation from the Islamic *Sharī'a.* He also believes that the Turkish elite socialized their descendents in a luxurious and libertine way which spoilt and weakened them to the extent that they passed their wealth to the Europeans by falling into the trap of their civilization. They lost their values and started to imitate the foreigners' ways superficially by gambling, racing and having foreign mistresses. They dropped their own languages[15] (Arabic and Turkish) and replaced them by European languages.

> Your sons haven't inherited your manners, as they did your wealth. They no longer have the gallantry to defend their honor and their name. They have no courage to fight. They are shameless and do not care to take revenge. A duel for them is a challenge uttered at night and retracted by day (al-Muwaylihī 1903 : 65).

[15] The ruling elite, although Muslims, did not even go to the trouble of learning Arabic. For example, Muḥammed 'Alī's Arabic was so bad that he used an interpreter, *Shaykh* 'Abdalla al-Sharqāwi (al-Jabartī, 1958; p. 682). Muḥammed 'Alī was not an exception; all the members of his family spoke Turkish and many of them never learned to speak Arabic well. King Farūq was the first ruler of the Muḥammed 'Alī family at whose court Arabic was spoken (Holt, 1968;p. 14). This phenomenon was not limited to the royal family, but extended to all Turkish families.

Hence, the radical change in the twentieth century is in the composition of the foreign community, the rise to dominance of the European and the supremacy of the European Western culture over the Egyptian. This change of the socio-economic and political structure of the society affected profoundly the attitudes and status of several indigenous groups.

First, the *'ulamā'* who used to occupy a leading position among the indigenous populace were now found occupying minor positions. In a modern state, established along western lines, the former eminent role of the *'ulamā'* as guardians of the *Sharī'a* was already changing, various traditional functions of the *'ulamā'* being taken over by secular institutions. At the beginning of the twentieth century the process of secularization and westernization was a topic of debate in Egyptian intellectual circles, where opposing views were expressed. A common view of this transformation along western lines was a general fear and mistrust of the consequences of that change. This change meant to some contemporary Egyptians a deviation from Islamic religious norms and submission to a foreign Western culture. This position was reflected in a interesting dialogue between 'Īsā ibn Hishām and the *Pasha* about the role of the national court which was a new introduction of the twentieth century:

Hishām: As for the national court, it is the jury that nowadays passes judgement on all disputes according to the Law.

Pasha: Humayyūni Law?

Hishām: The Imperial Law, for it is the Law of Napoleon the Emperor of France.

Pasha: And did the French return and submit you to their rule and sovereignty once again?

Hishām: No, it is we who submitted ourselves to their rule, for we chose their law to replace our *Sharī'a*.

Pasha: Do the rules of that law coincide with Islamic *Sharī'a* and pure Sunna? If not, then you are being ruled by other than God's prescriptions.

Hishām: This issue is debatable. *'Ulamā'* of the *Sharī'a* secretly and in their hearts agree that this Law is contrary to the *Sharī'a* and that to those who approve of it, the following Qur'an verse applies: "who do not judge according to what God has given, then these are the heretics". However once it came to public declaration, they announced it to be coinciding with the *Sharī'a*. One of the prominent *'ulamā'* declared when the law was published that this French Law is not contradictory to the *Sharī'a*. But this law does not provide penalty for . . . (many cases) which the *Sharī'a* has specified.

As for the Mixed Courts, whose judges were foreigners, they specialized in settling disputes between natives and foreigners and among foreigners themselves. These courts were mainly concerned with financial matters. . . . Most of the cases presented before these courts were inevitably judged in

> favor of the foreigner, stripping the Egyptian of this money and estate (Muwaylihī 1903 : 28–29).

The second group, whose status changed from one of prestige and wealth to one of powerlessness, were the merchants. Again, with secularization of the Egyptian society trading was taken over by foreign companies and institutions and the Egyptian merchants were left with the small scale internal trade. While the status of merchants was descending, that of the *effendī* (bureaucrat) class was rising. A common attitude in the society was the extra respect given to the government employee. An early twentieth-century bureaucrat, drawing a comparison between the status of a merchant and of a government employee remarked:

> " . . . the least tiring job is to serve the government and only those who lack foresight would prefer trading over employment in the government. To prove my point a bureaucrat can enslave any merchant with some money but the richest merchant is in need of the smallest bureaucrat in the government. Just observe the merchants in their circles. If you saw how they brag about the visit of a bureaucrat, or a talk to an officer, or a judge's greeting, you would know that government service has acquired such a high status in their eyes as well as in the eyes of the other classes of the society that . . . if a merchant is offered the choice between his trade, wealth, land and being a government employee he would choose the latter (al-Muwaylihī 1903 : 157).

The *effendī* strata came to the front as a result of the efforts to create a modern state requiring an increased number of civil servants. This group emerged from the educated sons of the *fallāḥīn*, craftsmen and merchants who received their education in new Egyptian schools or were sent abroad. In either case, it was no longer the formal traditional education of al-Azhar, but rather a western education. The prevailing attitude of this strata was an attempt to emulate western culture and to negate what was local, i.e. *baladī*. This attitude is critically recorded by Muwaylihī in a caricatural dialogue between two members of this strata as follows:

> First: Are you going to keep your promise to accompany me to our friend's to see the famous *baladī* dancer (belly dancer)?
>
> Second: Please excuse me, for it is impossible. First, this *baladī* dancing which *awlād al-balad* and the *fallāḥīn* enjoy, doesn't interest me. Second, I have invited "madmoiselle . . . " the famous opera singer for lunch in Azbakīya at 'Santi (a well-know European restaurant at that time). After that, we will go to Khān al-Khalīlī . . . and some of the old areas of the city for entertainment.
>
> First: How could you afford to go to these places? You said you had nothing left from your monthly salary.
>
> Second: I forgot to mention that we will have with us the lawyer and his friend the *'umda* (mayor).

First: How could those two agree to enter such foreign company when they don't know any foreign languages?

Second: Don't you know my dear fellow that it is the desire of the lawyer to accompany the judge, the *fallāḥ* (meaning the mayor) to imitate us; they are ever so eager to attend foreign gatherings however costly and useless they are.

First: Where did you buy that *kravat* (tie)?

Second: I didn't buy it "mon cher", it came with my clothes from my tailor in Paris. It's the latest fashion.

First: Have I told you the reason for the suicide of so-and-so's son?

Second: I know why, it was love.

First: No.

Second: Money?

First: No.

Second: Illness?

First: No, it's the new rage among Paris youth, and so he imitated them (al-Muwaylihī 1903 : 20–1).

These petty bureaucrats, by longing for a foreign style of life, were eager to rid themselves of all symbols of a local, i.e. *baladī* identity. Hence, a belly dancer, a local dress, Arabic speech, local concerns, are things that should be looked at disdainfully and be refuted. Hence the spread of westernization and modernization is no longer limited to the aristocratic elite but has extended to the petty bureaucrats.

One can conclude that a very negative attitude towards the identity of *awlād al-balad* prevailed among a large section of the society at the turn of the twentieth century. The collectivity identified as *awlād al-balad* in that period would be mainly local traditional merchants, craftsmen and the masses of the Cairene lower classes. These groups became powerless and ineffective in the political structure of Cairo.

CHAPTER TWO

HOW OTHERS VIEW IBN AL-BALAD

Given the radical changes that took place in the Egyptian society in the twentieth century, to what extent can we still discern a group identifiable as *awlād al-balad*? In everyday usage of the term, there exists an implicit image of a specific group which is characterized differently by different groups in Egyptian society.

The concern of this chapter is twofold. First, it will investigate various elements of the typification of the *awlād al-balad* in relation to the different classes[1] in the society. The class variable is a significant one due to the change which the 1952 revolution brought about in class structure. With the abolition of the aristocratic landed class, the limitation of land ownership, and the nationalization of large businesses, one might also expect a change in the status of the masses. Specifically, to be a "son of the country" *(ibn al-balad)* became a matter of pride, whereas to be a son of an aristocrat *(ibn al-zawāt)*, became one of shame. Due to this revolutionary dictum, and some of its positive practical results, one would expect to find a positive image of *awlād al-balad*. Yet empirical investigations have shown that there is still resentment in some eyes toward *awlād al-balad*.

Second, the discussion will attempt to reconstruct the various elements of the typification of *awlād al-balad* in order to ascertain the standard prevailing image, as conceived by the majority of persons interviewed. This will be done by elucidating from the previous survey the implied elements that constitute this typification in order to find out to what extent they are significant and essential to this image. One of the main reasons, therefore, for surveying the various elements and their significance in the image of

---

[1] "Classes" in this chapter is used in a broad context to differentiate between three socio-economic groups of Cairenes. The criteria by which different classes were distinguished are mainly socio-economic and educational. Thus the sample of upper class interviewees consisted of those who have university degrees and whose income is within the highest category of Egyptian society. Besides these criteria, the reputation of the person as being from an aristocratic family was taken into consideration. In this class we have famous doctors, ex-large-land-owners, members of the royal family and Egyptian aristocracy, big industrial businessmen, famous lawyers and engineers, and top level government officers. In the middle class come university graduates, as well as those who achieved average educational levels. Most government officials fall within this category, along with small merchants and owners of small enterprises. Within the lower class group are the working classes, whether industrial or craftsmen, servants, peddlers, or office-boys. The majority of this group is illiterate.

awlād al-balad is to get at the *specific contemporary collectivity* that is associated with them in the minds of the people. Hence analysis in this chapter is done at two levels that cut through each other. One level deals with variation according to class, but variation is explicitly mentioned only when it is significant. The other level deals with significant elements shared by all classes to reconstruct a typology of the collectivity of *awlād al-balad.*

1. Elements that Constitute the Image of Awlād al-Balad

Residence

Cairo is still specified as the particular urban location of *awlād al-balad.* Within Cairo itself, however certain groups are excluded from the collectivity. However, none of the interviewees would identify a Bedouin or Nubian as an *ibn al-balad. Ibn al-balad* was also sharply differentiated from the *fallāḥ,* the *Ṣa'īdi* (from Upper Egypt), the *Baḥrāwī* (from Lower Egypt), the *Asyūṭī* (from Asyūt, in Upper Egypt), the *Ṭanṭāwī* (from Tantā, in Lower Egypt), etc. Thus, since only the Cairene-born are *awlād al-balad*, it is understandable that none of those groups whose place of origin is outside Cairo would be considered *awlād al-balad.*

Although *ibn al-balad* must be a Cairene, he does not have to live in any specific part of Cairo to be identified as such. However, there was general consensus among the interviewees that *awlād al-balad* are found in *al-aḥyā' al-sha'bīyya* (folk quarters). The folk quarters most often associated with *awlād al-balad* by the respondents were al-Ḥusayn, al-Sayida Zaynab, Būlāq, al-Ghurīyya, al-Khalīfa, Bāb al-Sha'rīyya, Khān al-Khalīlī, Old Cairo and al-Muski. These quarters were described by some interviewees (especially those from the upper classes) as the slums of Cairo. But most interviewees pointed out that these quarters are old and traditional. Consequently, they maintained that *awlād al-balad* are found in these quarters, whereas one would not find an *ibn al-balad* in newer sections, such as Zamalek or Garden City, because these quarters are inhabited largely by foreigners and westernized Egyptians, who are characterized by a different set of values and life-styles. The respondents went on to say that not only are *awlād al-balad* characterized as dwelling in *al-aḥyā' al-sha'biyya*, but the inhabitants of *al-aḥya' al-sha'bīyya* are equated with *awlād al-balad.*

Education

Most of the respondents thought that an *ibn al-balad* could be either formally educated or illiterate. However, it was mostly the upper class group who equated *ibn al-balad* with the ignorant, even though some of them were aware of the spread of education among the lower classes. One of them remarked resentfully, *"awlād al-balad* nowadays are keen about educating their children. You see one who is only a porter but who wants his son to become a doctor".[2]

Most of the middle class interviewees who were university graduates or undergraduates said they would never describe a university graduate as an *ibn al-balad*. One expressed this as follows:

> *Awlād al-balad* may be educated but only to a level which would not exceed primary schooling. Once he becomes educated, the *ibn al-balad* is considered by his class as an outsider because he himself would negate his identity and consider this label as an insult.

Such contempt for the notion of an *ibn al-balad* as a university graduate was affirmed by several university-educated interviewees, who gave such examples as: "I once called a girl, a colleague of mine at University, a *bint al-balad*. She got angry and thought I was insulting her." However, in contrast, ignorance could also be considered by some interviewees as a delightful element, as one respondent remarked: "The *ibn al-balad* is not educated and this is part of his gay personality. The day he becomes literate, he will lose this kind of joviality and become dull."

Contrary to the previous conceptions of *ibn al-balad* as ignorant and naive, most interviewees (apart from the upper class group) thought that, although he might be illiterate, an *ibn al-balad* was highly knowledgeable about everyday life. It was often remarked that "an *ibn al-balad* learns from life; he learns from interacting with different kinds of people. Hence, his school is life itself." Or again, "The majority of the *awlād al-balad* are uneducated, but their instinct is very sharp;" "it is not essential that an *ibn al-balad* be educated; I knew of a car mechanic who used to speak three languages fluently without knowing how to read or write and this man was a real *ibn al-balad.*"

Some respondents explained that education is associated with the modern, western way of life, and that educated people adhere more to foreign patterns of behavior. As one said:

---

[2] This remark refers to the change that has taken place in the educational system. Before the 1952 Revolution, education was limited to those who could afford to pay the fees. Thus before 1952 it was very unlikely that a lower class person could afford to send his son to a university. Now, with free education, many of the lower classes are eager to have their children become university graduates. Another phenomenon is that the lower classes look at education as a means of social mobility. There is resentment now among some members of the upper classes that the lower classes are aspiring to be equal to them in occupation through education.

If an *ibn al-balad* is educated and at the same time adheres to the values of his class, then he is an *ibn al-balad*. But if he changes and becomes modernized, then he is no longer an *ibn al-balad*.

Religion

The majority of interviewees pointed out that whereas an *ibn al-balad* could be a Muslim or a Christian, he was mostly associated with Islam. Nevertheless, some of the upper class respondents were consistent in their notions about class structure:

> More Muslims are in this class of *awlad al-balad*, but if Christians are from lower classes and live in slum areas, then they are *awlād al-balad*.

One Christian from this group touched upon the question of Pharaonic Egyptian identity as opposed to Muslim identity in the following terms: "A Copt could be a real Egyptian but not in the context of an *ibn al-balad.*" Here the interviewee is referring to the concept of *ibn al-balad* as an index to Muslim Egyptian identity from which Copts can be excluded. It was often said that "the Christians are not as bold and courageous as *awlād al-balad.* They are overcautious, more tactful and diplomatic." Another interviewee remarked that "the Christian is not identified as an *ibn al-balad* because a Christian resembles and acts like a *khawāga.*"[3]

Occupation

While almost half the interviewees indicated that *awlād al-balad* could be employed in any kind of work, the majority conceived of them as doing independent, non-government work. Some interviewees were hesitant as to whether certain jobs were unique to *awlād al-balad,* but all interviewees from all classes agreed that butchers and *baladī* coffee-shop owners are always *awlād al-balad.* This image was so firmly fixed in the minds of the interviewees that, when asked why a butcher should be an *ibn al-balad,* they could give no explanation other than simply asserting that "he *must* be an *ibn al-balad!*" A few remarked that these jobs required contact with many people, and required alertness and quickness, which are qualities identified with the *ibn al-balad.*

Strata

An *ibn al-balad* as a Cairene is distinguished from certain others in the

---

[3] *Khawaga:* foreigner. For a more detailed explanation see Introd. p. 1, n. 1 and Chapter IV.

society. The *fallāḥ* was sharply distinguished from the *ibn al-balad* in the following representative quotation:

> The *ibn al-balad* is someone living in Cairo; he is *midardaḥ* (implying alertness, intelligence, etc.) and not like those who come from rural areas.

Implied in this remark is the idea that the *fallāḥ* is stupid compared to the *ibn al-balad.* This comparison was repeated in the following remarks: "The *fallāḥ* is ridiculed by the *ibn al-balad";* "the *fallāḥ* is submissive, cowardly and suspicious; hence he is not an *ibn al-balad."* However, some interviewees from the lower class group, who are themselves originally *fallāḥin,* contradicted the majority:

> The *fallāḥ* is the *ibn al-balad*, because his father and grandfathers are *fallāḥīn* – that is, real Egyptians.

In contrast to the lower class group's concept, if an upper class respondent identified the *fallāḥ* as an *ibn al-balad,* it was simply because he saw both as being of the lowest class of Egyptian society.

Another strata[4] that was sharply distinguished from *awlād al-balad* by most interviewees was that of the *effendī* (bureaucrats). The upper class group rejected the identity of an *ibn al-balad* as a bureaucrat on the basis of status. To them a bureaucrat dressed in a suit, and thus he could not be an *ibn al-balad.* On the other hand, the lower class group objected to identifying an *ibn al-balad* as a bureaucrat because to them the concerns of the bureaucrat were different from those of the *ibn al-balad.* As one of them pointed out:

> The bureaucrat cares a lot about his appearance and dress, on which he spends a lot of money, while the *ibn al-balad* spends more on food. For example, while the bureaucrat might bring just one chicken to his family, the *ibn al-balad* would bring four. Also, a bureaucrat would make four meals out of one kilo of meat, while an *ibn al-balad* would cook it all and eat it in one meal.

This example implies more than merely a different order of priorities in household management or in different ways of cooking. Cooking in large quantities is a sign of hospitality, which is itself a traditional value. Hence, the interviewee was referring here to the *ibn al-balad's* traditional way of doing things as well as his adherence to Egyptian values.

---

[4] In Arabic "strata" or "class" means *ṭabaqa.* Strata/class is used here in the context of *ṭabaqa* at the "common sense" level, with no sociological specificity intended. The interviewees may use such a term as "strata" or "class" to distinguish the *ibn al-balad* from the *fallāḥ*, or the *effendī*, without necessarily intending the analytical socio-economic meaning of class.

The major objection of all classes to the identity of the bureaucrat as an *ibn al-balad* was in relation to the different character traits displayed by each. Some respondents explained this notion in the following terms:

> The *ibn al-balad* is not as diplomatic as the bureaucrat or the educated because the nature of bureaucratic work is different. The bureaucrat has superiors; hence his livelihood is in their hands. This encourages him to compromise and to be a hypocrite.

The worker stratum of the society is not so sharply differentiated from the *awlād al-balad* as is that of the bureaucrat. Some interviewees, mostly from the middle class, denied that workers (particularly factory workers) are *awlād al-balad.* To them, the craftsman is more of an *ibn al-balad* because his job is in the *baladī* quarter, whereas the factory worker has to leave his residential quarter to get to his work. They also assumed that the effect of industrial work on the worker makes him acquire different (i.e. more modern) characteristics as well as a different outlook. The workers in the sample, however, disagreed strongly and pointed out that it is the workers who are real *awlād al-balad,* and one of them asserted that "even if the worker has to leave his quarter and live beside his factory, still he is an *ibn al-balad* because his new neighborhood is that of workers who are also originally *awlād al-balad.*"

Class and Wealth

Most of the respondents identified the *ibn al-balad* as of lower middle class location, meaning that group which preserves the traditional Egyptian values more consistently than any other. As some interviewees pointed out, once an *ibn al-balad* becomes too rich it is no longer possible to classify him as an *ibn al-balad,* since he would probably change his residence as well as his style of life, and this in turn would affect his traditional values. Furthermore, "it is not so much the *amount* of wealth that one possesses as what one does with it which identifies one as an *ibn al-balad.*" For example, a coffee-shop owner, or a butcher, could become very rich but still follow the customs of the group, such as staying in his quarter, helping and cooperating with the neighborhood, preserving his family relationship as well as friendship ties – in short, keeping his identity as an *ibn al-balad*. On the other hand, with his wealth, he might move from his own quarter to a new one, forget his origins, despise his old neighbours and friends, try to become assimilated into the new environment and negate his original identity. In such a case, he would no longer be considered an *ibn al-balad*. This description of the *ibn al-balad* was mainly held by the middle class group of respondents. The upper class group, however, conceived of him as very poor, and identified him with the lowest economic strata in the society. None identified him as an upper class person, or, as the latter is often called, *ibn al-zawāt.* This denial of a high status to the *ibn al-balad* continues to be his most distinctive characteristic, as we have frequently noted. Contrary to these groups, most of the lower class respondents did not classify the *ibn al-balad* as belonging to any class in particular, because he did not have to be either rich or poor.

It is interesting to note not only the status of the *awlād al-balad,* but also the manner in which the different classes of interviewees identified themselves in relation to the *awlād al-balad.* No one from the upper class sample would classify himself as an *ibn al-balad.* However, a few of the upper class group expressed the notion that they might wish to be *awlād al-balad:* "I have many things in common with the *awlād al-balad,* yet they would not accept me as one of them." Or: "I wish I could be considered an *ibn al-balad* because although unconsciously I used to reject this group, lately I have come to feel that I am also rejecting my Egyptian identity."

On the other hand, many interviewees from the middle class (specified by the majority as the class constituting the majority of *awlād al-balad*) hesitated as to whether they would consider themselves *awlād al-balad* or not. Only half of them conceived of themselves as *awlād al-balad.* All of the interviewees of the lower class, however, conceived of themselves as *awlād al-balad,* saying, "of course we are *awlād al-balad.*"

From the above survey it can be seen that all interviewees agree that the *ibn al-balad* is *not* an upper class person, that is, not *ibn al-zawāt.* This has become standardized in colloquial Arabic where the latter is polar to *ibn al-balad.* In brief, the upper class group sees the *ibn al-balad* as lower class. The middle class group see him as middle class, although most were hesitant about this identification. Finally, the lower class group see him as belonging to themselves – that is, as *awlād al-balad* and not to a class.

Physical Appearance

In people's minds there is a concrete image of the *ibn al-balad* in terms of his external appearance, attire, way of speaking, tone of voice, kind of dialect and special vocabulary, including the invectives he uses. A number of interviewees cited the famous actor, Muḥammad Riḍā in the character of *Mu'allim* Sharārā, as an example of a typical *ibn al-balad* with all his mannerisms, dress and speech. Both the upper and middle class groups identified the *ibn al-balad's* attire as consisting of a *gallābīyya* (long gown), a headdress and a walking stick. Those from the lower class said that he could be dressed in any attire, even in a European suit. A general characteristic of his appearance mentioned by only some of the upper class group was that he would usually be shabby and dirty.

The *ibn al-balad* was also described by many as having a peculiar manner of speech. The dialect he employs is a special kind of urban colloquial Arabic that differs from rural dialects as well as from those of other social strata in Cairo itself. His special style of talking was described by many respondents in the following terms:

> He speaks a little nasally. He draws out words and lengthens the ends of sentences. He swallows some of his syllables. For example, he says *walla* instead of *wallahi* (by God). His speech is full of puns, and words are used figuratively. He usually garnishes his speech with proverbs.

Some of the interviewees cited several common expressions as unique to the *awlad al-balad*. For example: *balā 'afya* (don't get me wrong); *wa lā' mu'ākhza* (pardon me); *'ālayyā al-na'ma* (may God's grace go against me); *'ālayyā al-ṭlāq* (may I be divorced, that is, if what I am saying is not true); *ya mīt misā'* (O hundred evenings); *nahārna ful* (our day is roses). The latter, when used in greetings, has the meaning, "You've made our day as beautiful as roses." Other typical expressions are: *ya gamīl* (O Beauty) and *mal'ūn abū al-dunya* (to hell with the world).

Several interviewees identified the *ibn al-balad* as the one who usually calls those older than him by certain titles such as "father of so-and-so" *(abū* Muḥammad) or "mother of so-and-so" (*'um* Muḥammad). Those somewhat younger than he are referred to as "brothers" *(akh)*, and those very much younger are called "boys" *(wad).*

The *ibn al-balad* was characterized by many as using the most vulgar invectives in public. But, in many contexts, he is using insults in a complimentary way, such as when he wants to praise the cleverness of a person, and says, "He is quite a man, but the son of a whore." Furthermore, harsh insults are not always meant to be so, such as when a mother addresses her son with "Oh, damn you!" Otherwise, and in general, the *ibn al-balad* is described as pleasant in his speech, and prone to talkativeness.

Virtues and Attributes

There are certain attributes that are particular to *awlād al-balad* in the context of a specific collectivity. As noted above, one attribute of the *ibn al-balad* is that he adheres to Egyptian traditions. Some interviewees even equated the term "traditional" with *awlād al-balad,* or the *baladī* people:

> Not all Egyptians are *awlād al-balad. Awlād al-balad* are a special kind of people of the old days. They are the *baladī* people.
>
> The term refers to a person who follows the ways of life of our forefathers.
>
> It is used of the person whose way of life does not differ from that of the old days.

Ibn al-balad is one who represents our old Egyptian tradition.

Most interviewees other than the upper class group described *awlād al-balad* as very religious: they are the ones who frequent the mosques nowadays, and are the ones who are very particular in carrying out the main edicts of Islam, such as praying, fasting, pilgrimage, and alms. It has also been pointed out that they are the ones who retain such traditional Islamic values as generosity, cooperation, helpfulness, charity and sharing. The upper class group, however, maintained that the *awlād al-balad* are superstitious rather than religious.[5]

The two most significant and outstanding attributes of the *awlād al-balad* as seen by most interviewees are *shahāma* (gallantry) and *fahlạwa* (cleverness). Another major attribute is masculinity. Many interviewees described the *ibn al-balad* as "the person who is manly," or "the person who is virile." Some described him as extremely fatalistic.

Although joking is generally a typically Egyptian trait, it is outstanding among *awlād al-balad*. Most interviewees described the *ibn al-balad* as a jolly person, one who is always surrounded by a group with whom he jokes, and one who makes fun of everything, even himself. The *awlād al-balad* have a special kind of humor called *k'afya*: a specific word (such as "garden" or "mother-in-law") is chosen and then two or more persons enter a sort of contest using the word chosen as the theme of their jokes. This type of humor depends on a person's alertness and quick-wittedness in using puns and figurative speech.

Another trait of the *ibn al-balad* mentioned by a number of respondents is that he never keeps his appointments. It was explained that, to an *ibn al-balad,* time is not a strict matter of minutes, but is flexible and limitless. One exemplified this notion by saying: "When they give a time for meeting, they usually say, 'We will meet in the morning, or at noon, or in the evening.' This means that it will not bother any of them if the person comes a few hours earlier or later."

---

[5] This notion of *awlād al-balad* being religious in a mystical or superstitious way seems to contradict what Max Weber noted as the tendency of artisans, craftsmen and middle class people to incline toward a rationalistic, ethical view of life. (Weber, 1969).

2. The Typification of Awlād al-Balad

In the following summary there are two sets of elements in the typification of *awlād al-balad.* One is related to their social status and the other relates to certain personality and cultural traits.

Stratification is associated with place of residence and education. Residence as an element in the typification of the *awlād al-balad* is a significant and essential one. *Al-aḥyā' al-sha'bīyya* are not only the places where *awlād al-balad* reside, but also all dwellers of *al-aḥyā' al-sha'bīyya* are *awlād al-balad.* Variations arise only in relation to the meaning of the label itself. The term *al-aḥyā' al-sha'biyya* seems to be a recent one which came into vogue when the 1952 Revolution put emphasis on the *sha'b* (people), or folk.[6] It encompasses more than its literal meaning (folk quarters) and implies, for example, the slum areas which are found in all cities and towns in Egypt. It also denotes *baladī* quarters, where *baladī* (local, folk) people reside, and it incorporates medieval Cairene quarters as well. The formal and linguistic terms do not differentiate between these various meanings, but the people themselves in everyday usage of the term do seem to differentiate. For example, the upper class group of interviewees used it to mean slum areas, whereas the majority of interviewees were merely specifying medieval Cairene quarters such as the *al-aḥyā' al-sha'bīyya* in which the *awlād al-balad* reside. Furthermore, there are those who would be considered *awlād al-balad* by all previous criteria, but who live outside these quarters. Yet the interviewees' own impression of where the traditional classes live most frequently specified the old parts of Cairo.

In these quarters there are slums, but we cannot say that all *al-aḥyā' al-sha'bīyya* are slums. The appearance of some of these quarters has not changed for centuries; some of the street plans are the original ones of Cairo. The streets in these quarters are divided into *ḥārāt, darb 'uṭaf* and *zuqāq,* which probably follow the original divisions.

In contrast to the element of residence, education was not thought of as an essential element in classifying a person as an *ibn al-balad.* Education was mainly associated with the way of life that the educated person leads, and how much he is influenced by Western patterns. The *ibn al-balad* is not necessarily either illiterate or educated. However, a few interviewees not only judged him as ignorant person but asserted that his jovial character results from his ignorance. Indeed, this aspect has been adopted in the mass

[6] *al-aḥyā' al-sha'bīyya*: literally folk *sha'bīyya* quarter. The term has been commonly used since the '40's. The term *sha'bīyya* was first used by the media but has now infiltrated into common colloquial language. The media's current preference for this term results from their wish to avoid the usage of a value-laden concept such as *baladī.*

media and exaggerated. Such naiveté and ignorance, for example, have become the main theme of the television serial comedy, *'Ukāsha 'Umāshā* (1971), in which the hero is an illiterate *"mu'allim"* who tries to use literary Arabic about which he is clearly ignorant, so that he grossly misuses it in hilarious ways. The whole humor of the serial was based on the *ibn al-balad's* use of the "literary" language revealing thereby his ignorance of terms and syntax.

Religion, like education, is not an essential element in typifying the *ibn al-balad* since most of those who negated the identity of the Christian as an *ibn al-balad* rejected it more on the basis of different character traits each displayed rather than on his faith.

Nor is occupation a significant element in identifying one as an *ibn al-balad;* the characteristics that pertain to some types of work (such as the independence of non-government work) are more essential than the job itself. Exceptions to that are specific jobs such as butcher and coffee-shop owner, and some traditional work patterns, where the job itself makes one an *ibn al-balad.* This strong association between *awlād al-balad* and these occupations might be due to the effect of the mass media, since in films and television the *ibn al-balad* is usually presented either as a butcher or as a coffee-shop owner. It may even be that these jobs were the ones that native Egyptians specialized in, just as Greeks in Egypt were specialists in the grocery and bakery trades. Also it might be due to the role of the butchers in popular revolts in the eighteenth century and the close association of this group with the *awlād al-balad* and the protective role they played in the popular quarters.

Usually the butcher, the *baladī* coffee-shop owner and those in traditional free-enterprise such as trading in food stuffs, are addressed by the title *mu'allim. Mu'allim,* as a title of address, is associated with traditional occupations as well as with folk quarters, and therefore is closely associated in people's minds with *ibn al-balad*. The two significant roles associated with *awlād al-balad* are that of *ḥashshāsh* (hashish addict) and of *futūwa* (tough guy). The common conception is that the *hashish* trader is a *mu'allim* and it is in folk quarters that hashish circulates. The *ḥashshāsh* as a jolly person seems to be particularly characteristic of the *awlād al-balad.*

The *futūwa* exemplifies another set of character traits which are associated with the *awlād al-balad,* namely strength, and awareness of one's strength and masculinity. In addition to this association, the *futūwa* has played an important role in the social structure of Cairene quarters.[7] How-

---

[7] This role will be dealt with in detail in Chapter III.

ever, since most of the interviewees were not fully aware of the original structure of these quarters, they limited the role of the *futūwa* to that of a thug (*balṭagī*) and included it in their typification of the *ibn al-balad*.

The *ibn al-balad* was singled out as a specific stratum in Cairene society as distinguishable from such other strata as the *fallāḥ* and the *effendī*. It is obvious that the main distinctions between the *fallāḥ* and the *ibn al-balad* are different character traits. Since the *ibn al-balad* is a Cairene, he cannot be a *fallāḥ*, and yet several interviewees asserted that the *fallāḥ* is an *ibn al-balad*. For the outsider (especially if he is an upper class person), the *fallāḥ*, as well as the *ibn al-balad* occupy the same status as the lowest class of the society. The interviewees who are themselves from the lower class identify the *fallāḥ* as an *ibn al-balad* on a cultural basis, that is, they share with the *ibn al-balad* similar values and attitudes towards life.

Those who viewed the *fallāḥ* as an *ibn al-balad* thought of him in the general context of the term, that is, as the real Egyptian, who preserves the values of the society. But when the term *ibn al-balad* is used in the context of a collectivity identified by locality, it usually relates only to an urban group.

The bureaucrat is another segment in Egyptian society that is sharply distinguished from *awlād al-balad*. Unlike the *fallāḥ*, the *effendī* does not share the values of *awlād al-balad*. It seems that the *effendī* strata symbolizes certain modern notions of a life style which opposes the conception of the strata of *awlād al-balad*, thought of as being very traditional. But the bureaucrats are particularly and sharply distinguished from *awlād al-balad* because they display different character traits.

This difference in character traits can be illustrated by examining two caricatures which have been used in the press to represent the Egyptian. One is of *al-Miṣrī Effendī*, who is clad in a European-style suit and a *tarbūsh* and carries prayer beads; the other is of an *ibn al-balad* in his *gallābīyya*. In explaining the difference between the two, Rakha, who originated the caricature of an *ibn al-balad*, said:

> In the year 1929 the caricature of *al-Miṣrī Effendī* was born in the magazine *Rūza l-Yūsif*. This caricature symbolized the good and submissive person who is passive and fatalistic and who, in the face of calamity, calls for God's help saying, "Damn those who have done me injustice." In the year 1941, the chief editor of *al-Ithnayn* magazine held a meeting with the editorial staff of *Dār al-Hilāl* (the publishing house), in which it was decided that the caricature of *al-Miṣrī Effendī* did not, and should not, symbolize the Egyptian, because it represented the lowest class of government official, that is the *effendī* class, or petty bureaucrats. They decided that the personality of an *ibn al-balad* represented a more independent and emancipated personality and one which really represented the Egyptian.

Compared to the *fallāḥ* and the *effendī*, factory workers are more closely associated with *awlād al-balad*. This association reflects the notion that these workers are mainly urbanites who usually dwell in *al-aḥyā'al-sha'bīyya* as *awlād al-balad*. It seems that living in a specific quarter imposes on its inhabitants certain patterns of behavior, attitudes and values. To many interviewees it is these patterns and values that are essential in identifying one as an *ibn al-balad*. In ranking *awlād al-balad* in terms of status and wealth, there was a good deal of variation in responses, but, as mentioned previously, most of the respondents specified *ibn al-balad* as belonging to the lower middle class income bracket.

Another significant and essential element in the typification of *awlād al-balad* is their physical appearance. The details of the *ibn al-balad's* dress and the mannerisms of speech are concrete in people's minds. The special emphasis on that particular element might again be due to the influence of mass media. In some Egyptian films and television programs this aspect is even exaggerated to such an extent that one would probably never encounter living persons who spoke in a similar fashion. The distinction of *awlād al-balad* in terms of occupation, education and status was rather vague in the minds of interviewees, but the personal and cultural characteristics were more significant.

There are a number of virtues that mark one as an *ibn al-balad,* but the most outstanding ones mentioned by the interviewees are *shahāma* (gallantry), conservatism, *fahlawa* (cleverness), masculinity, and joviality.

Shahāma, an Arabic term that has no exact equivalent in English, is gallantry mixed with nobility, audacity, responsibility, generosity, vigor and manliness. *Shahāma* also implies helpfulness and readiness to bear responsibility. As a man endowed with *shahāma*, an *ibn al-balad* is always ready to volunteer help without being asked. A common illustration of this attitude, cited by many interviewees, is that the *ibn al-balad* is the one who interferes in settling a quarrel without knowing the persons involved. As for those he knows, such as his relatives, friends and neighbors, he takes to heart their cause even if they are in the wrong. He feels that to have *shahāma* he must stand by them and not let them down. It is often said in folk talk, "he is *gada',*" someone you can depend on, "solid," meaning that he is manly and has *shahāma*.

An instance cited illustrative of this attitude was of an *ibn al-balad* who was taking the bus to the *al-Ghūrīyya* quarter and who asked the ticket-collector to stop the bus before the station. The ticket-collector refused and a fight ensued. In the bus there happened to be two people from the same district as the *ibn al-balad* who immediately interfered to support him and together they forced the ticket-collector to stop the bus. Another illustration of this attitude, cited by many respondents as a common occurance, is that if somebody asks directions, several *awlād al-balad* might volunteer information and would even go with the enquirer all the way to his destination. A third aspect of *shahāma* is related to hospitality and generosity in a way that is unique to the *awlād al-balad*. One bureaucrat interviewee, in describing what the thought was the *awlād al-balad's* conception of hospitality said:

> The *ibn al-balad* is keen to behave as a *shahm* person; hence he has to be very receptive to his friends. For example, he would insist on paying the bill for the group with him in a coffee house. Among us bureaucrats, we would simply have paid each one for himself, but an *ibn al-balad* would think our behavior improper and unmanly. It is a scandal for him to behave in the way we would.

Such behavior is an act of *gad'ana* (a manly act) and he is very keen to identify himself with this, as someone who knows his duty and is eager to fulfil it.

Fahlawa is another colloquial term with no precise equivalent either in English or in classical Arabic. It implies such qualities as sharpness, cleverness and alertness. Some interviewees described *fahlāwa* as native wit: a kind of intelligence that springs from experience rather than formal education. From continuous interaction with all sorts of people, a person becomes knowledgeable about human behavior. For example, an *ibn al-balad* will adapt his way of talking to the person with whom he is interacting. When he speaks to a Greek, the long-time residents of Egypt, he changes his dialect and imitates them so that they may understand him. He understands very quickly and learns other languages very easily. One informant pointed out that most of the workers in the butcher shops, groceries and bakeries in Zamalek, where a number of Russians had moved, learned to speak adequate Russian in a very short while.

The *fahlawī* has the alent of convincing others of his ideas. As a merchant such a person is capable of making the customers buy something he never intended to get. *Fahlawa* can also mean feigning ignorance of things that one is familiar with in order to fool others. The *ibn al-balad*, as pointed out by one informant, usually practices his *fahlawa* on those who are not from his group or class, such as the *awlad al-zawat* or the *khawagāt*. Another manifestation of *fahlawa* is to feign understanding when one does not understand, or ignorance when one does. As the saying goes, "I'm swallowing it but of my own free will."

The Egyptian sociologist, Hamīd 'Ammār, in his book *Fī Binā' al-Bashar*, assumes that the term *fahlawi* denotes the cultural pattern of the Egyptian nationality ('Ammār 1964). This assumption is too general and his argument is not well substantiated. In the present investigation the attribute *fahlawa* emerges as a characteristic of the *awlād al-balad*, as a specific group, and does not pertain to Egyptians in general. The *fallāḥ*, for example, is not considered *fahlawī*.

Some aspects of ʻAmmar's description of the term *fahlawī*, however, are in accordance with many interviewees' conception of it. ʻAmmār explains that, undoubtedly, the first aspect of *fahlawī* behavior is the ability to adapt quickly to various situations and the ability to distinguish the most desirable behavior demanded by a given situation. It is usually said that the *fahlawī* is one who can mix with the "red djinn" and at the same time live with the angels of heaven and earth, meaning that he can interact with any type of person. This he can do at will and without effort. Thus, the *ibn al-balad* with his quick adaptability is able to accept new things without confusion or hesitation.

The ability to adapt quickly is characterized by two features: first, flexibility in assimilating what is new, and second, the capacity to hide true inner feelings. This notion falls within the expression, "it's just talk," which means that one does not really mean what one says nor is one going to be bound by one's words.

ʻAmmār explains this pattern of behavior as the outcome of political conditions in Egypt, specifically, the numerous foreign rulers the Egyptian people have been subject to. Consequently, a superficial means of confronting such situations is essential for survival in constantly changing and unpredictable conditions (ʻAmmār 1964 : 81–82).

A major attribute of the *ibn al-balad* is his masculinity. He is particular about his behavior and his appearance. He never shaves his moustache, nor plucks his eyebrows. He will not walk in the street arm in arm with a friend nor talk in a soft manner or tone. Such behavior is not permissible from an *ibn al-balad*, and he would define it as being feminine or even homosexual. This strong awareness of his manliness is expressed in his relation to others, especially his wife. Most of the interviewees thought of the *ibn al-balad* as the person who has complete authority in his home and who keeps his home and his wife completely under control. The role of the wife is therefore limited to that of mother and housekeeper. She should be submissive, obedient, a good cook and an excellent housekeeper, as well as a comfort to her husband. She should not leave the house without his permission, nor receive a stranger in his absence. Her main duty is to follow his orders. She has limited rights under him, all of which are in the economic domain. This concept of the relation of the *ibn al-balad* to his wife coincides with the description of *muʻallim* Kirsha in the novel *Zuqāq al-Midaq* by Nagīb Maḥfūẓ. When *muʻallim* Kirsha's wife quarrelled with him for his immoral behavior, Nagīb Maḥfūẓ described the man's reaction in the following terms:

> It is very strange that he sees himself (*mu'allim* Kirsha) as always being right. He was astonished and saw no reason for her interference or objection. Is it not his right to do what he wants? Is it not her duty to obey and be satisfied as long as her needs are fulfilled and her provision plentiful? (Maḥfūẓ, 1963 : 82).

The *ibn al-balad* is thought of as a very jealous and tough person, both attributes being considered expressions of masculinity. As a powerful man he prefers a submissive wife. Unless the man is strong and powerful and can control his wife, she will not respect him, nor be submissive to him. A strong man is respected and loved both in the family circle and in the community. This notion of the *ibn al-balad's* masculinity is expressed by Nagīb Maḥfūẓ in the following terms by *mu'allim* Kirsha's wife:

> What an impatient man! He spends whole nights outside his house without being bored, yet he gets annoyed from two minutes' talk with her. But still he is her man in front of the people and God: he is also the father of all her children. It is strange that with all the mistreatment of her, she cannot despise him or neglect him. He is her man and her master. She is never tired of correcting and restraining him whenever he is inclined to immoral behavior. She is even proud of him, proud of his masculinity and his position in the quarter and his strong control over all his colleagues (Maḥfūẓ, 1963 : 81).

As a man, the *ibn al-balad* is solely responsible for the economic welfare of the family. He would not permit his wife to work because this would be a slight on his masculinity. It is often said to a working woman, "If your husband were a man he would not let you work." As long as the *ibn al-balad* can support his family nobody can interfere with him, but if he is no longer able to earn a living, his rights over his family become limited.

A major aspect of this notion of masculinity is sexual virility. To be a man is to be sexually strong. An *ibn al-balad* is seen as being very much concerned about his sexual potency. If he loses it he is no longer considered a "man." The worst insult and the most bitter sarcasm that can be levelled against an *ibn al-balad* is that relating to his masculinity and virility. Most jokes center around sex. Sex to an *ibn al-balad* is very basic and many attitudes and behaviorial patterns have developed around it. For example, specific kinds of foods are eaten to strengthen the sexual capacity, such as eggs, pigeons, *farīk* (green wheat), and *ḥalāwa ṭaḥīnīyya.* Nagīb Maḥfūẓ describes the effect of such food in the following terms:

> It is a pan of *farīk* in which pigeons are put and mixed with the powder of *gawzat al-ṭīb*. It is eaten at lunch after which he (al-Sayyid Salim) drinks a cup of tea every two hours. Thus its effects last for two full hours of pure pleasure (Maḥfuẓ, 1963 : 73).

Some of the jokes cited by the interviewees reveal the importance of virility and its effect on women. Among themselves women boast of their husbands' potency and the number of times they have intercourse weekly, as well as the length of intercourse. As mentioned by some interviewees, the *ibn al-balad* chooses fat women as partners because he considers them sexually attractive. Hence the *bint al-balad* seeks various means to be sexually attractive. If she is thin, she will seek the spice merchant's advice on how to become fat. The *ibn al-balad* believes that he takes *ḥashīsh* mainly for sexual reasons, not only to make himself more virile but also to make it possible to prolong intercourse. Some say it is because the women are circumcised and cannot respond quickly. Another expression of the importance of sex can be illustrated in the sphere of family relations. Usually, it is not easy for a woman to ask for divorce and she has to bring her demands to the family or to court. One of the widely accepted causes for divorce is her accusation that her husband is not a man, that he is sexually impotent.

There are certain characteristics such as generosity, sharing, and a passive fatalism that are not particular to *ibn al-balad*, but belong to a set of common Arab-Islamic characteristics. They are, however, accentuated among the *awlād al-balad*. The *awlād al-balad* are described as extremely fatalistic. An *ibn al-balad* depends on God in all his deeds and actions. Nagīb Maḥfūẓ, in his story "Khān al-Khalīlī," sums up in the expression "to hell with this world" a complete outlook on life. This is expressed by *mu'allim* Nūnū in the following terms:

> God protect us. It is wiser not to worry. Leave your cares and laugh. Worship God, for the world is God's world. What is done is done by Him and what happens He brings about. The end is His, so why think over things and be sad?
>
> To hell with the world – this cry does not mean cursing or blasphemy, for can we curse it in deed as we do in words? Can we be indifferent and laugh at it? When it reduces you to poverty, when it strips you naked, and when it makes you miserable and hungry? Believe me, life is like a woman – she turns her back on the one who goes on his knees to her and accepts the one who beats and curses her. My approach to the world and women is the same. I rely on God first and last. Sometimes things go badly and God does not send things our way. Nobody knows what the children will eat and I do not have the price of a *hookah*. Yet I just go on singing, cursing, and joking as if the children were my neighbor's children and it is my enemy who is hard up. Then everything goes well. Be happy, Nūnū. Thank God, Nūnū. Zaynab, go and buy some meat. Run off, 'Aysha, and get some melon. Fill your belly, Nūnū and your children eat up (Maḥfūẓ, 1965 : 46).

The previous attributes constitute significant elements in the typification of the *awlād al-balad*. Some of these attributes conform to the negative or positive stereotyped image one group has of the other.

Conclusion

The *awlād al-balad* as an identifiable group are described as Cairenes who dwell in *al-aḥyā' al-sha'bīyya.* They display certain character traits such as *fahlawa*, alertness, intelligence, quick-wittedness, masculinity, joviality, independence and extroversion, that distinguish them from other strata in the society, such as the bureaucrats and the *fallāḥīn.* Their major attributes are those that pertain to and spring from traditional values such as *shahāma, gad'ana,* fatalism, generosity and sharing. Apart from these attributes, there are certain characteristics that distinguish them, such as their manner of dress, appearance and speech.

Although all the above elements are essential to the typification of the *awlād al-balad* as an identifiable group, some elements are emphasized more than others. From examining the various elements, the most strongly emphasized is that of residence; second is character traits; third, type of occupation, and finally, some suggestion as to their place in the social stratification.

It seems that the cultural elements that relate to a specific style of life, certain values and character traits are more essential in identifying the *awlād al-balad* than a class structure. Hence we can conclude that the cultural elements in the contemporary typification of the *awlād al-balad* that relate to a specific style of life, certain values and character traits are more prevalent and important in identifying one as an *ibn al-balad.* The groups that are associated with that style are mainly residents of folk quarters. Residents of these quarters vary in status. In economic terms they range between middle, lower-middle, and lower classes. But the interviewees' conception of the social and economic status of the *awlād al-balad* varied according to their own status.

The upper class respondents identified the *awlād al-balad* as the lower class of the society, dwelling in the most slum-like areas of greater Cairo, or even in the villages. They wear *gallābīyya* and are characterized by the kind of jargon and insults they use. They are also characterized by their ignorance, illiteracy and dirtiness. Therefore, to this group the most significant elements in the typification are those of physical characteristics and their low status. The few members of the upper class group who deviated from this negative image of the *awlād al-balad* indicated that they had had some personal contact or close relations with typical *awlād al-balad* characters.

It is obvious that this negative typification emphasizes only superficial elements such as dress and unacceptable language. The image lacks detail and refinement. This can be explained by the large gap that has existed between classes, and especially the complete alienation of the upper classes from the masses. Hence the upper class knowledge of other social groups depends on stereotyped notions. They look down on anything that is native and Egyptian, that is, *baladī*. They have internalized some of the foreign notions and attitudes towards the indigenous population. The derogatory attitude of the foreign elite towards the *awlād al-balad* in the eighteenth century has been transmitted to the contemporary *awlād al-zawāt*. It seems that the *awlād al-zawāt* were eager to identify themselves with the *khawāga* stratum of the society, to copy their behavior and unconsciously to internalize their attitudes towards the *awlād al-balad*.

It is interesting to note that although this negative image of the *awlād al-balad* is beginning to fade with the passing of what used to be identified as an aristocratic class, members of the middle class are beginning to pick up elements of the former upper class group's conception. Moreover, some of the negative elements of this typification are still used in the mass media to identify the collectivity.

The hesitation of the middle class group to identify with the *awlād al-balad,* their ambivalent attitude toward them and their negation of that identity seems to indicate changes in class image. Even with a socialist ideology, the middle classes have upper class aspirations. The middle class group in their upward mobility are borrowing the class symbols of a higher group. A negative image of the *awlād al-balad,* or even a rejection of that identity, is becoming one of the symbols of elite status. Hence, while the elite were trying to get rid of the symbols of an aristocratic position, the lesser or middle classes in particular were picking them up and identifying with them. The ambivalence of the middle class group's position (in which they identified *awlād al-balad* as middle class, yet didn't identify themselves as *awlād al-balad*) emerged from the new situation of a socialist revolution that implemented socialist slogans and emphasized the role of the masses. Hence, while the formal revolutionary leadership of the bourgeois class held to a socialist ideology, the middle class base had an elitist aspiration and was unconsciously (or otherwise) copying and imitating the attitudes of this class.

In contrast to the position of the middle class group, we find that the lower class group remain consistent in their image. They see themselves as being of this group and are proud of that identity. Hence it seems that it is basically a lower class group which is associated with the style of life and values of the *awlād al-balad*.

From the above typification, it is clear that its most concrete element is that of residence. Hence the next step in the investigation is to select from these quarters a sample of interviewees in order to arrive at the self-image of the *awlād al-balad*. But before turning to an analysis of the self-image, it is necessary to discern the common characteristics of these quarters that are part of the identity of the *awlād al-balad*.

CHAPTER THREE

THE COMMUNITY OF IBN AL-BALAD

As a group, *awlād al-balad* have been described as inhabitants of certain Cairene quarters, mainly al-Darb al-Aḥmar, Jamalīyya, Bāb al-Sha'rīyya, Būlāq, and Mīṣr al-Qadīma. Each of these quarters will be found in medieval descriptions of Cairo. An Egyptian's conception of these quarters today is that they form the *baladī* (local, traditional) Cairene community. This "common sense" conception of the community of *awlād al-balad* coincides with what Janet Abu-Lughod has termed "traditional urban." She categorizes the Cairene population into three main types or models: the rural, the traditional urban, and the modern or industrial urban. She defines traditionalism in a general way:

> Traditionalism refers primarily to the persistence of economic activities, forms of social relationships, and systems of values which were once typical within the Cairo of a hundred years ago but which, since the advent of the twentieth century at least, have been increasingly challenged by several ways of organizing production and sale, regulating identity and behavior, and setting definitions for the good life (Abu-Lughod 1971 : 219).

According to Abu-Lughod, the heart of Cairo's traditional urbanism lies in those very districts which have been settled the longest, that is, the quarters of the medieval city. However, not all of today's residents of these communities descend from inhabitants in the middle ages or even a century ago. The communities are changing constantly. While a sizeable number of rural migrants come to settle, at the same time many of the older residents leave their quarters for more modern ones. But despite this mobility we find that whatever traditional activities still survive in Cairo are found chiefly in these old quarters. Therefore, the traditional model, with its cultural and physical boundaries, corresponds to the community of *awlād al-balad* as described at the 'common sense' level.

The medieval Cairene quarters, in which the *awlād al-balad* dwell, share certain common physical, demographic, cultural and social features that associate the *awlād al-balad* in people's minds with the traditional style of life.

1. Physical and Demographic Features

These quarters are described as comprising mostly old buildings and have, in particular, most of the prominent religious structures located in them. However, the community of *awlād al-balad,* while having the longest history of settlement, is not far from the new and modern zones of the city. Hence a common physical feature of this community is the coexistence of the old and the new. Medieval mosques stand side by side with twentieth century mosques, large paved streets with alleys, and new buildings with old ones.

Medieval Cairene quarters have been divided into districts (*ḥārāt*) which emerged from and supplemented the original divisions of the community. Some of these *ḥārāt* are small dead ends and lanes with backyards in which children play and women meet and chat. In the past the buildings of each small lane usually belonged to and were occupied by only one family. But now there are a number of families in each house, some of the larger flats being divided into three or four apartments with each apartment being shared by two or three families. The division within the apartment is sometimes only a wooden partition. In one of these buildings there can be as many as 250 people, with about 25 persons sharing one apartment. This pattern of accomodation is not unique, but rather it is becoming a common feature of these quarters. For example, the number of families who share flats in al-Darb al-Aḥmar represents about 30% of the district's total number of families (al-Gam'īyya al-Miṣrīyya 1970 : 83).

The original *ḥāra* in medieval Cairo was not only a physical administrative unit but also a social unit. Its inhabitants were unified by ethnic, religious and/or occupational characteristics which segregated them physically and socially from other subgroups of the city. Today, the *ḥāra* is no longer unified on the basis of ethnicity, religion or occupation, but more on the fact that the same lane is shared by several neighbors, who view themselves according to their place of origin, either mainly as *awlād al-balad* (Cairene) or as *fallāḥīn* (rural migrant). In some *ḥārāt* there dwell a number of Upper Egyptians *(ṣa'īdis)* and people from the desert oases *(waḥātiyya).* They are predominantly of the Islamic religion. There are, furthermore, very few foreigners.

Another distinctive feature of each of these communities is that population shares certain demographic characteristics that sets it apart from other sections of Cairo. Cairo as a whole is one of the most densely populated cities in the world. It was estimated that in 1977 Cairo had a population of almost 8 million. According to the sample survey of 1966 it had a population of 4,964,004, with a density of 19,594 persons per square kilometer. The medieval Cairene quarters were the major pockets of population density in the city. The quarters corresponding to those in medieval Cairo had an estimated population of 277,577 persons, approximately 6.6% of the total population of the city, and a density of 77,875 persons per square kilometer. In spite of this density the area is full of ruined and demolished buildings which are often used as refuse dumps.

Much of the housing in the area is in a state of extreme deterioration. Forty-five percent of the buildings are in bad condition and thirty-seven percent of them are substandard. Fifteen percent of these buildings have neither water nor electricity. The region is also deficient in medical and recreational services. Furthermore, these quarters receive many if not most of the rural migrants to Cairo.

The level of education in these areas is low and the ratio of illiteracy is high compared to that of Cairo in general. At least fifty percent of the population in these areas is illiterate, but among its women alone illiteracy is over sixty percent. Of those who are literate only a very small proportion have ever reached university level. The occupational distribution in these quarters is related to the standard of education. The percentage of those who work in professional occupations is much lower than the percentage of those who do manual work. The most common occupations, in which about half of the working population is involved, are crafts, manual labor, factory work, and selling. This is a high percentage compared to the 32% who are involved in these occupations in Cairo as a whole. Approximately 61% of the working population of medieval Cairo work within the area. Due to the degree of illiteracy and the type of occupations these people are involved in, the range of income is naturally low (al-Gam'īyya al-Miṣrīyya 1970).

2. Culture of Awlād al-balad as Awlād al-ḥitta

Dwellers of these *ḥārāt* identify themselves as *awlād al-ḥitta*. Literally, *ḥitta* means place, but in the sense of one's territory or neighborhood. It has physical and social boundaries which may extend from a small alley to a whole quarter, depending on the number of people with whom an *ibn al-balad* or *bint al-balad* identifies him-/herself.

> "A *ḥitta* is both a geographic and a social entity. It is a strictly subjective term whose social and geographical boundaries are identified only by its residents and the people of the bordering *hitat*. People residing in the same *ḥitta* do not necessarily know each other or have face-to-face relationships, but they do consider themselves bound by vicinal ties. They have an *esprit de corps* which is most visible at times of weddings, deaths and fights" (Nadim 1975 : 43).

Within the *ḥitta* there is constant interaction between men and women. Women are not secluded from men. The contiguity of the houses plus that of the living units brings together individuals who are sometimes mere neighbors and have no kinship ties. This influences social relations in these *ḥārāt* and gives rise to certain unique patterns of interaction. Some of the obvious patterns that emerged in mixed group gatherings are the permissiveness and talkativeness of women, and the informal intermixing of age groups and sexes.

Young boys and girls have an active role in any discussion. They express an open and joking attitude toward elderly persons of both sexes. They often contradict their parents' opinions frankly, or disregard them completely. A most striking feature of these gatherings is the lack of inhibition in relation to sexual issues and how married women in particular center their jokes and sarcasm around sex.

Awlād al-ḥitta use certain titles of address. Elderly people are addressed by the title *'umm* (mother) or *abū* (father). Another common title of address for elderly people is *ḥagg* or *ḥagga*, indicating that the man or woman has made the pilgrimage to Mecca. In addition to these general titles of address there are specific occupational titles such as *mu'allim* (male chief) or *mu'allima* (female chief). Those who supervise and control certain merchandise are mainly addressed by this title. As for those who work in crafts or industry, they are addressed by the title *'usṭā* (expert or teacher).

The *awlād al-balad* in these *ḥārāt* are recognized by their traditional dress, which is mainly the *gallābīyya* for men and the *milāya laff* (square black overwrap) for women.

The *bint al-balad* in the *ḥitta* attracts attention by the manner in which she dresses. While the *milāya laff* itself is a black overwrap, the dress worn under it is bright and colorful and also cut in a rather seductive way: neither completely closed nor blatently open. The dress might have a low cut decolleté but with ribbons that appear to close it. The *bint al-balad* will wrap the *milāya laff* in such a way that her midriff and hips are clearly outlined to show the shapeliness of her figure. The overwrap allows part of the body to show, like a bare arm, while the other one is covered. There are certain accessories which go with the *milāya laff.* One is a head scarf which is either all white or one brilliant color, embroidered on the edges with large flowers hanging from it in a fringe. This scarf is supposed to cover her hair; however, it is usually left loose enough so as to slip continuously half off, necessitating frequent stops to adjust it and the *milāya.* Thus in the middle of the street a *bint al-balad* can take off the scarf, tie it again around her hair, then re-wrap the *milāya* around her body, all of which allows her to perform a series of alluring gestures by which to attract the attention of passers-by.

Another accessory is the high-heeled slippers or claq that she customarily wears, rather than shoes, so that her walk can be accompanied by an attractive sound. Or else she might wear flat slippers, but with an ankle bracelet which also produces a tinkling sound. She might also wear gold bracelets on her arms. For her make-up, the most important item is the black *kuḥl*, or eye-liner.

Although the *milāya laff* is the most common dress in these areas, many of those who wear it (especially the younger generation) use it interchangeably with western dress, depending on the occasion and place. Such particular concern for mannerisms of dress among the women of these areas emerges from the great value placed on femininity and their concern to be sexually attractive.

Another indication of the coexistence of the old and new is reflected in their accepted values in which, for example, modern medical treatment is used side by side with folk remedies. Part of the common conception that the dwellers of these quarters are traditional is due to the kind of beliefs they hold, such as their practice of folk remedies for various ailments and diseases.[1] They believe in saints and their healing powers. The saints' important role in these areas is reflected in people's celebration of their birthdays, and visiting holy men's tombs on various other occasions. People usually distribute gifts or 'make vows', which could be either money or food, for the poor living nearby, in return for the anticipated saintly blessings. Each *shaykh* is famous for his particular kind of *baraka.* Hence the saint's status varies according to his or her "speciality." For example, *shaykh* al-Sha'rāwī is supposed to be especially potent in curing mental diseases: Sayyida Nafīsa specializes in eye diseases; there is *shaykh* Mughāwrī for curing sterility, *shaykh* Yaḥyā for solving personal problems, and so on. People in these areas interact with saints as with living people who are capable not only of rendering services but also of inflicting punishment and revenge on one's enemies.[2]

---

[1] Folk remedies are numerous and they are tied to certain folk diagnoses. For example a man who is incapable of sleeping with his wife (impotent) is diagnosed to have been shocked or terrified suddenly. If a woman is sterile or is delayed in pregnancy then she has been exposed to *mushahra. Mushahra* is defined as a "supernatural harm caused to individuals in vulnerable states by others persons' violation of taboos." (Kennedy 1967 : 1). Violation of these taboos would cause *mushahra* which under these circumstances prevents pregnancy unless traditional curative measures are taken. Folk remedies are varied and numerous and are usually prescribed by an elderly woman, fortune teller, or the midwife in cases of pregnancy and delivery. See John Kennedy for detailed information on this issue (J. Kennedy 1967).

[2] Sayyid 'Uways, an Egyptian sociologist, had made an interesting study analyzing a sample of letters sent to one of these *shaykhs* and the type of services demanded from them ('Uways 1965).

Resorting to folk remedies is more common in certain afflictions than in others. In these areas they are aware of the superiority of modern medicine in organic diseases and it is only in cases where they cannot afford to pay for medical services or when the modern treatment fails to cure that they turn back to the folk remedies. In psychological or psychic disorders they believe that their own folk methods, in particular the *zār*,[3] to be far superior. The *zār* is not only a ceremony designed to rid the patient of evil spirits but is also an occasion for the women of the whole *ḥitta* to gather and celebrate. Other common ceremonies in the *ḥitta* are related to the life cycle such as *subū'* or the seventh day after a child's birth. Rituals related to the dead and to visiting the tombs are adhered to very strongly in these areas as well.

3. Roles of Awlād and Banāt al-Balad

The residents of the popular quarters engage in activities similar to those undertaken by the inhabitants of the same quarters two centuries ago. Some of them, too, are occupied in jobs related to the new industrial society, in big factories or in government institutions.

It is in these quarters that one still meets the traditional water carrier, the *'er'usūs* (local syrup) carrier, cart drivers and peddlars of local food. Craftsmen and artisans who comprise a large percentage of the inhabitants carry on their work in the midst of their own homes assisted by their wives and children. There still exist numerous *baladī* coffee houses in which coffee, the and the *shīsha* (water pipe) are served. In these coffee houses, until recently, folk singers would recite stories of Arab heroes accompanied by the plaintive tones of the *rabāba*. The coffee shop owner, the butcher, and those engaged in free enterprise like the *mu'allim,* are all associated with roles of informal leadership in the *ḥitta.*

A large number of women occupy certain roles that reflect the prevailing pattern of the community, that is, the coexistence of the old and the new. While some women still carry on certain jobs such as *ballāna* (one who does depilation), *dāya* (midwife), fortune teller and *mu'allima*, many women work in factories, or as tailors, dressmakers, shop assistants, nurses or government employees, depending on the amount of education they have received.

---

[3] The term *zār* refers both to a ceremony and a class of spirits. The purpose of the *zār* is to cure illness through contact with the possessing spirits which cause such maladies (See Kennedy 1967).

In these quarters one comes across *banāt-al-balad* who keep haberdasheries others who sell *ṭa'mīya, fūl* and salad on carts, while others help their husbands sell fried meat balls. A very common scene in the *ḥārāt* is to find women who open small *baladī* coffee houses of just two benches, where tea and coffee as well as the *gōza* (a long-stemmed pipe) are served. Several women fortune tellers might sit in the streets close to a *shaykh's* tomb with their clients around them in a circle.

Inside the houses many women take an active role in the preparation of their husbands' wares. Here there are many men who have migrated from the oases and specialize usually in *fūl mudammis* (a bean dish) merchandise. Their women are daily occupied in cleaning and washing the kilos of *fūl* that have to be cooked in huge pots and circulated to the individual sellers. Similarly engaged are most of those involved in any food production. The woman prepares and cooks the food while the man does the marketing.

Another important role in these quarters is that of the *ballāna*. The *ballāna* usually works in a *baladī* public bath as well as going monthly to female clients in their houses to bathe them and do depilation. Bathing in a *baladī* public bath involves not merely washing with soap and water. The *ballāna* oversees a rather lengthy procedure. First, her client sits for a time in a *maghṭas* (a large tub) which is filled with very hot water. Then follows the stage of *takyīs* ("gloving") in which a sort of glove made from very harsh wool is used. The *ballāna* wears the glove and rubs every part of the *bint al-balad's* body. The heels are rubbed with a pumice stone. After the gloving stage the client rubs down with a *līfa* (coarse natural sponge) and soap. The process of bathing in a public *baladī* bath usually takes at least two hours. Depilation and bathing are usually done every two weeks.

In addition, the *ballāna* performs certain rituals in relation to occasional bathing, that is, bathing for purification after childbirth and the bathing of the bride. Also, she helps in dressing and ornamenting the bride on the night of the wedding. But nowadays, as one of them said, "couples refuse our help and think this is a *baladī* (old-fashioned) way, that should not be used." But generally the *banāt al-balad* use the public baths and the *ballāna* for some of the rituals connected with childbirth. Otherwise, as one young *bint al-balad* said, "We *banāt al-balad* go to the hairdresser when we need to and it is only the villagers who use the *ballāna* to bathe them."

Not only is the *ballāna's* role changing but so too is the class of her client. Fifty years ago the public *baladī* bath was an essential institution since private houses had neither baths nor tubs. Only the very elite could afford to have tubs similar to those of the public baths for their personal use. Therefore the *ballāna* in the public bath also used to attend to women of the upper classes, but now only the lower classes go to them (Amin 1950).

Another role that is common in these quarters is that of *dallāla*. The *dallāla* is a sort of middle-woman who knows the merchants of various commodities and who has close personal contact with the women of the quarter. She is thus aware of the needs and tastes of various women and she buys a variety of women's goods from the shops and sells them mainly to women confined to their homes. Nowadays, she buys and sells an even greater variety of goods. An interesting development in the role of the *dallāla* is her buying produce wholesale and selling it on credit to those who cannot afford to pay outright in cash.

There is no job differentiation according to sex in these quarters in certain roles, such as the *mu'allim*. The *mu'allim* or *mu'allima* are mainly butchers, *ḥashīsh* merchants, coffee shop keepers or influential merchants in the market. They direct quite large and successful enterprises. Traditionally, the *m'allima* has in her shop a large special chair or a *baladī* sofa on which she sits and smokes a *shīsha*. She is coquettish and gives much care to her appearance, adorning herself with expensive jewelry. Her dress, however, is a man's *gallābīyya,* which is complemented by a rather masculine air. She takes part in quarrels like any man, and disciplines anyone she dislikes with a beating.

The most significant role of the *mu'allim* in these quarters in the first decade of the twentieth century was that of the *futūwa*. By definition the *futūwāt* are young men, although found among them in these quarters are a few *futūwa* women. These young men and the occasional woman were, and to some extent still are, responsible for the protection of the locality against outsiders. The *futūwāt* in these areas are informal leaders whose power is derived largely from their identity as *awlād al-balad* who share certain obligations toward the people of their neighborhood. We may classify the role of the *futūwa* in these quarters into two types: one is the *ibn al-balad* type, the other is the *baltagī* (thug) type.

There are certain qualities which mark the *futūwa* as a leader – qualities shared also by the people of these quarters. Among these traits are *'ayāq*, cleanliness, intelligence and alertness. But the basic quality which sets off the *futūwa* from others is his physical strength, still acknowledged today by nicknames such as 'Urābī, drawn from the famous Egyptian nationalist hero (1879–81); al-Fahl al-Kabīr, the big animal; Zalaṭ, the stone; al-Ḥisān, the horse. The *futūwāt,* including the women among them, are physically imposing. For example, 'Azīza al-Faḥla was described by those who knew her as follows:

> I saw 'Azīza al-Faḥla, who was head of all the *futūwāt* in al-Mighārbilīn. A giant lady who possessed extraordinary strength. Around her arms were tons of gold bracelets. A blow from her hand was enough to knock any man to the ground. A blow from her head would split a stone. She was married to a man called al-Faḥl al-Kabīr. He used to

> support his wife in any quarrel but this was rare because 'Azīza was always capable of gaining victory by herself. By becoming one of 'Azīza's followers, I learned my first lesson in *fatwana,* that is, the brave acts of the *futūwa* (El-Miligi : 13).

But physical strength must be accompanied by bravery. The young man 'Abdūn, an admirer of a certain *futūwa* known as al-Duqma, set out to cultivate those qualities that would permit him to join al-Duqma's clique of supporters. Thus he was advised:

> "Be careful, don't get near him with this mien, this odor or this oily garment. Be like pure water and try your luck."
> It was also said to him, "Our *futūwa* loves beauty and purity and is unique among the *futūwāt.*"
> 'Abdūn was convinced that the way to al-Duqma was easy. Thus he went to the public bath "to change his skin" in the tub, prepared a new *gallābīyya* and *bulgha* (slippers). While busy renewing himself thus, one of his friends asked, "What is it, 'Abdūn? Are you thinking of marriage?" 'Abdūn told him his secret, but his friend said, "Cleanliness alone doesn't interest al-Duqma; he also loves to listen to tales."
> 'Abdūn's secret became known, and everyone knew that he was preparing himself for *al-fatwana*. Several took the initiative to advise him, one of them saying, "Cleanliness is important, tales are important, but for al-Duqma bravery is more important than either."
> "Bravery?"
> "Yes. Also, be careful not to arouse his jealousy, for otherwise he will be angry rather than pleased with you."
> "How can I compromise between the one and the other?"
> Another person said, "Strength is also important; you have to prove your strength. You have to prove that you are capable of striking the final blow and also enduring them, however hard they may be. At the same time, you have to prove to him that your strength is not comparable to his" (Maḥfūz 1975).

This passage refers not only to the basic characteristics of *futūwa* but also to the process by which one might set about to become one.

The *futūwa* of the *ibn al-balad* type is usually recruited from the people of the *ḥitta.* He is generally employed in one of the local trades such as a butcher, a coffee shop owner, a dealer in food stuffs, a cart owner, or a scrap merchant. *Mu'allim* Yūsif, a *futūwa* of the 1920's who later dictated his memoirs, refers to his upbringing in these terms:

> I was born in the streets of al-Ḥusaynīyya. My father and mother dwelt in *ḥarāt-al-ḥuṣr.* I was brought up among lovers of abuse and scorners of school education. They were the advocates of education by the meat cleaver. In fact, most of the inhabitants of al-Ḥusaynīyya are butchers who kill and skin but of course don't read and write. My father, who owned a butcher shop, sent me to the *kuttāb.* For three years I attended the *kuttāb* only by continual spanking. I left it after

> learning how to write my name and read two lines in the newspaper in an hour or two. My father used to tell me, why bother about the *kuttāb,* are you going to be a government employee, or an *abukātu* (lawyer), or catch a wolf by the tail? What you need is a couple of calves and a shop, and God will take care of the rest. I submitted to God's wish and took off the tarboush and put on the turban, changed my shoes for slippers and became a *baladī* lad. . . . I joined a clique, and we used to go every night to a wine shop, or *gōza (ḥashīsh)* party" (Yūsif 1925).

Part of the social identity of the *futūwa* relates to the network of activities he is involved in. The *futūwa* in his *ḥitta* is mainly seen as the protector of the neighborhood against rival *futūwāt* or any other outside opponents. Most of the problems the people bring to the *futūwa* relate to work situations, or those that emerge from the traditional style of life and the values attendant to it. Tvpically, people interact on a personal basis with no formal contracts, bills, or receipts. In these arrangements a man is "tied by his tougue," that is, bound by his word. In this way if someone borrowed money from his neighbor without a receipt and refused to pay it back or even denied that he had borrowed it, the *futūwa,* after an investigation, could force him to return the money. Some clients may take commodities from shopkeepers, promising to pay later, but continually postpone payment or refuse it altogether. The merchant would then seek the help of the *futūwa.* The *futūwa* might even end a dispute by himself paying the amount at stake.

The *futūwa* would also look after the welfare of the community as a whole. For example, he would protect the *ḥitta* from thieves, or help supply the *ḥitta* with scarce commodities, such as oil or kerosene, to spare the people from black market prices. In the economic crisis of 1942, a certain *futūwa* used to procure the kerosene allotment for his whole *ḥitta,* protect it during delivery, and then distribute it equally throughout the *ḥitta* without taking any fee.

The *futūwāt* have also been engaged in safeguarding public morality and the reputations of the local inhabitants, especially those of the women. In the 1930's, in quarters known for prostitution, such as al-Azbakīyya, the local protectors were referred to insultingly by outsiders as the "*futūwāt* of females".

Charity to the poor was and is an important attribute of the *futūwa* and one of the basic values that confers prestige and fame. Wealth in itself does not make one popular, but rather what one does with it, how much one spends on the poor, on others, or how much one spends to feed others.

From the above it is clear that the *futūwāt* work in financially relatively rewarding jobs that set them above the average wage-earner and which allow them to be generous. 'Azīza al-Faḥla, the most renowned female *futūwa,* in al-Migharbīlīn, worked as a dealer in food stuffs such as cheese, eggs, fruits, vegetables and beans. From this she earned enough to enable her to buy about ten houses in the *ḥitta*, a coffee shop and several other shops. Similarly, the earnings of the butchers and coffee shop owners were such that they could afford to be more generous than most people in these areas.

One of the *futūwa's* most clearly defined duties is that of protector of his people during ceremonial occasions, such as marriages and circumcisions. Part of the marriage ceremony consists of a procession, or *zaffa,* in which many of the male residents of the *ḥitta* gather. In the 1920's, if the *zaffa* of the bridegroom had to move from one quarter to another, it could proceed only with the permission of the *futūwāt* of that *ḥāra.* Anyone in the locality sponsoring a ceremony would usually seek the protection of the *futūwāt* of the *ḥāra* to safeguard the ceremony from rival *futūwāt* or any other trouble-makers, or to guard the ceremony from the depredations of the local *futūwa* himself, had he been neglected by his clients. It is common, even now, that weddings witness quarrels in the folk quarters. Rival *futūwāt* usually seek such occasions to express their animosity, and the gathering of the people of one neighborhood in that of another often leads to friction. Protection by the *futūwa* is thus essential for the continuity and orderliness of the ceremony. At the same time, the *futūwa's* ability as an attacker and defender is established and adds further to his reputation.

As a leader, the *futūwa* does not work alone. His prestige in the *ḥitta* depends upon the number of his supporters. The *futūwa* is usually identified as someone who has *'azwa* (from *'aza*, meaning to trace back). Strictly speaking, *'azwa* means having the support of one's ancestry, but for the *futūwa 'azwa* refers to the number of his living supporters. The potential supporters come from various categories that are referred to as "followers" *(atbā'),* "boys" or "lads" *(subyān),* a clique *(shilla)*, and "those who stand for you" *(maḥāsīb* and *mashādīd).* A common threat or challenge today is, "I will beat you and those who stand for you." Thus, part of Aziza al-Faḥla's strength lay in the fact that she had ten strong brothers, a strong husband, about thirty men who worked for her, "boys" in food merchandise, a clique of women sellers who accompanied her in the market and were her *maḥāsīb,* and finally all the people of the *ḥitta* who were her potential *mashādīd.*

It was common to find serveral of the prestigeous *futūwāt* in businesses that involved a large number of apprentices, his *subyān* being simultaneously a major source of support. Being a *futūwa* was not a negligible business, and it was occasionally profitable, but profits and prosperity came from the profession itself rather than from the *futūwa's* extra-professional role as protector and strong arm of the weak.

The *futūwat* within and among different localities are in constant competition to assert their supremacy, their quarrels taking on the proportions of feuds. To end a feud between two equally renowned *futūwāt* is difficult because any appeal for reconciliation would be answered by the saying, "We are *gad'ān* (tough and brave) and men do not give up their revenge." In a quarrel it is expected that a *futūwa* will beat and be beaten by others. But to be attacked and run away, or not hit back, would identify a *futūwa* as a "woman" *(mara')*, which is the most humiliating insult he could receive. Reconciliation of rival *futūwāt* is done as diplomatically as possible to lessen the tension between the parties and the shame of the loser. The most important thing is to preserve the honor and manliness of each and to assert that they are both *gad'ān.*

It is also common that the *futūwa* is in more or less constant conflict with the local authorities. His fights, for instance, frequently lead to the voluntary or involuntary "closing of shops" in the *ḥitta* as shop owners want to keep themselves and their merchandise out of harm's way. Entire streets or quarters may close down during, or in anticipation of, a brawl, if a renowned *futūwa* starts a fight. Moreover the number of shops that close is an index of his prestige and power; therefore if compliance is not spontaneous, he will, in the interests of his own reputation,. have to force their shutters down. While the local authorities treat these as illegal acts, the *futūwa* sees them as legitimate expressions of *gad'ana* and bravery.

If someone acts improperly in the *ḥitta,* the *futūwa* may take it upon himself to correct that behavior. If the police intervene, the *futūwa* is likely to take on the police as well. In some instances of particularly brutal police intervention, the *futūwāt* have responded by attacking the police station and the policemen. The result is that *futūwāt* are frequently taken into custody and imprisoned. However, there is no stigma attached to being jailed, and the *futūwāt* proclaim that they are not criminals but *gad'ān*, and that "prison is for the *gad'ān*." Correspondingly, they consider the authorities weak, corrupt and easily fooled, and thus contrive to outwit them and their systems. Yusif al-Ḥaggāg, in his memoirs, describes an incident in which he escaped six months' imprisonment after having beaten up and wounded a couple of men in a quarrel:

> While walking with the policeman to prison, I planned to run away. To put the policeman at ease, I started giving him one cigarette after another, and then I told him what a scandal it was for a *futūwa* like me to walk like a prisoner with handcuffs, so I called a coach and we rode in it. In the coach I disjointed the handcuffs with a coin. In front of a coffee shop I asked the coachman to stop. The policeman asked why we were stopping, I said, "Just to take care of you for your help (meaning to get him some money)." The policeman's face relaxed, and I left him in this state and went home. Do you know why I es-

> caped? Afraid of prison? Never. I just wanted to prove to them (the government) that they are stupid (Yūsif 1925).

This anecdote highlights the fact that in all his actions the *futūwa* depends not only on his strength but also on his intelligence and craftiness.

The opposition of the *futūwa* to officialdom is intensified when the authorities are foreign. The means of opposition vary, however. In opposing one another they rely mainly on the personal assets of strength and skill in fighting, particularly in the use of clubs, knives and swords. But in opposing authorities with overwhelming means of coercion at their disposal, the *futūwāt* must rely on deception. During the British occupation of Egypt (1882–1954) the *futūwāt,* assisted by the people of their quarters, resisted the British by such acts as throwing hot water on them, killing drunken soldiers at night, and digging holes in the paths of soldiers and then covering the holes with straw. They exploited British ignorance of local customs. Once, during a periodic search for weapons, the British came across a sword in the house of ʿAzīza al-Faḥla. They were about to arrest her when she explained that the sword was not a weapon but a symbol that she used in the *zār.* The British accepted this explanation and left, ignorant of the fact that swords have no place in such ceremonies.

In their resistance to the British authorities, there is no indication of group action in which the *futūwāt* of different localities united with the people of the quarters in a manner similar to the *zuʿr* in their resistance to the French in the eighteenth century. Rather, resistance on the part of the *futūwāt* in the twentieth century took the form of individual patriotic acts. ʿAzīza al-Faḥla, for example, used to lure rural migrants away from British employment during the Second World War by offering them higher salaries. She also used to attack and beat those whom she suspected of collaboration with the British.

In general, the political awareness of the *futūwāt* was not as sophisticated as that of the educated classes. They cooperated with explicitly nationalist groups, such as the students, because they found the students to be brave young men willing to stand up to the British. Yusif al-Ḥaggāg, in his memoirs recalls the 1919 uprising:

> I was walking in al-Ḥusaynīyya when I met a large group of *effendī* (gentlemen) students and religious students (from al-Azhar) who were shouting and demonstrating. On asking about the reason for the clamor, they answered that the British had imprisoned Saʿd Pasha (the Prime Minister). I asked who Saʿd Pasha was. They said he was asking the British to leave Egypt, but they put him in prison. I said he is then *gadʿa* and immediately I joined the demonstration. To tell you the truth I discovered that these students are real men. Among them were daring ones who just threw themselves upon the British to fight them. I and my clique joined them, and when the British tried

> to capture one of them, we tried by all our means to release him (Yūsif 1927 : 3).

The other polar type that is associated with the role of the *futūwa* (in the opinion of the most interviewees) is the *balṭagī* (thug or tough). The *balṭagī* might be either from the locality or from outside, but he is not closely associated with the people of the *ḥitta*. He shares with the *futūwa* physical strength and skill in fighting. Achieving these core qualities and hence the identity, *fatwana* becomes for the *balṭagī* a source of profit or a crude expression of power.

The sorts of activities in which he engages are different from the *futūwa* of the *ibn al-balad* model. He is not associated with the protection of the interests of the *ḥitta*. On the contrary, he abuses the people of the *ḥitta* by taking ransom on certain commodities that they sell, or simply by taking goods that he wants without payment. In other cases he is ready to sell his skill and will accept payment to beat someone up, wreck a ceremony, or close a shop or club. He does not abide by the norms and values of the people, and his leadership is imposed upon the quarter by exploitation, force and fear. At the same time the *baltāgī's* reputation for brutality protects the *ḥitta* from outsiders. Thus he at the same time exploits the people of the *ḥitta* while he protects them from the abuse of others.

The *futūwa's* role at the beginning of the 20th century was characterized by certain personal qualities that could not be transferred or inherited. The role is rooted in the specific rights and duties that he asserts or must perform. How he maintains his dominance in any given locality differs widely. As an *ibn al-balad*, the *futūwa* is a working man, occupied mainly in traditional and profitable jobs that require several apprentices. He is not formally educated and he adheres to the traditional style of life. The *futūwa's* resources differ in degree but not in kind from those of his supporters, that is, the people of the *ḥitta*. He simply acquires more of what they have or would like to have. The *futūwa* is pre-eminent; he is the strongest and the bravest. The major issue is what he does with his strength. A strong man who abuses his power for his own interests is not a real *futūwa,* he is a traitor. A real *futūwa* is one who uses his strength to protect those in need. Accordingly, whatever assets he has should be shared. His relation with the people of the *ḥitta* is reciprocal. He provides them with tangible goods as well as protection, and in return he receives non-tangible benefits such as prestige and status. His dominance in the *ḥitta* is based not on brute force but on authority and quasi-institutionalized rights and duties. In contrast, the *balṭagī's* leadership is based on power, and he asserts his dominance by sheer force. His relation with the *ḥitta* is one of avoidance rather than reciprocation, and his protectees change their status from client to victim.

As protector, the *futūwa* is not alone in his locality. Other potential protectors or informal leaders comprise the *ibn al-balad* himself, who although not necessarily a skilled fighter, may be a merchant, craftsman, or shop owner, and with some advantage in financial resources is prepared to undertake leadership functions. The *'ulamā'* of the *ḥāra* are potential protectors as well, but how effective their role has been since the beginning of the twentieth century is moot. It seems that unless they were financially well off their leadership was limited. In all instances, however, accompanying the broad changes in the composition and occupational structure of urban society in the last fifty years, has been a profound transformation of the bases of protection. The personalized and individualistic style of the *futūwa* has been partially overwhelmed by more anonymous groupings associated with factories, the sprawling public bureaucracy, or associations based on social level and wealth.

Within the *ḥāra* both the social milieu and the protection functions that the *futūwa* undertakes have changed considerably. Successive waves of rural migrants, especially during and since the Second World War, have swamped some of these older quarters of Cairo. In place of the relative homogeneity that existed prior to the twentieth century, one may today find side by side in any neighborhood a mixture of upper Egyptians (*Ṣa'īdīs*), lower Delta Egyptians (*Baḥrāwīs*), people from the oases, and the original Cairenes, the *awlād al-balad*. The co-existence of these different groups, with different life styles and occupations leads, minimally, to a fair degree of social distance among the component parts of the neighborhood and sometimes to open conflict. One must add to this two other factors. The first is the enormous overcrowding now prevailing in medieval Cairo with all the tensions it produces. The second is general overall decline in the standard of living for many strata of these quarters.

CHAPTER FOUR

THE SELF IMAGE OF IBN AL-BALAD

All the interviewees from Medieval Cairene quarters labelled themselves *awlād al-balad.* Most of them were keen to express their esteem for and devotion to this identity in the following terms: "I have the honour to be an *ibn al-balad.*" To them all dwellers of medieval quarters were *awlād al-balad*, but those identified as such should possess certain distinguishing characteristics.

1. The Typification of Ibn al-Balad Among Dwellers of Medieval Cairene Quarters

From a survey of these characteristics one finds certain items emerging as essential for the typification of the *ibn al-balad*. Medieval Cairene quarters have a high percentage of illiteracy and a very low percentage of university graduates. The very low percentage of highly educated persons in these areas is due not only to the fact that few people complete their studies but also to the exodus of those who become educated and leave their original quarters. This pattern seems to be common to the extent that those who *are* highly educated and *remain* in the quarter are identified as the real *awlād al-balad.* An example of the educated *ibn al-balad* is Bayram al-Tūnisī, one of the greatest composers of the Egyptian folk ballad. Many interviewees referred to him as a genuine *ibn al-balad* despite his high education and world wide travels. He had never permanently moved away from his old neighborhood right up until his recent death. For the educated to be identified as an *ibn al-balad* he has to have been brought up in these quarters; however a formal education or lack of it is not a necessary element in the typification of *ibn al-balad.* Religious affiliation is also not essential. In the opinion of the majority of *awlād al-balad*, he could be either a Muslim or Christian. This was justified by pointing to the similar ways of life which Muslims and Christians lead in these quarters. This was pointed to in such terms: "The Christians here in the *ḥitta* are hardly noticed. They sit like us in a *baladī* coffee house eating a dish of *fūl* just like any Muslim." Therefore, in this case, residence is more significant than religious affiliation.

Although the *awlād al-balad* specified certain jobs as pertaining specifically to the *ibn al-balad,* yet occupation in itself is also not an essential element. Tradesmen and craftsmen only symbolize certain essential attributes and values associated with the typification of the *ibn al-balad.* They touch upon a certain way of life where a man is not alienated from his community by his job. His work is integrated into his everyday living and he has a good measure of control over his livelihood.

The association of the *ibn al-balad* with craftsmen and tradesmen is partly due to the high status these groups used to acquire. As one craftsman put it:

> Khān al-Khalīlī craftsmen are skilled workers who earn a lot and spend a lot. They are open-handed and generous. They have their own special gathering places such as *baladī* coffee houses which offer specific amusements, e.g., *Tawāshih* or songs on the *rabāba* (a musical instrument used especially in accompanying the narrator of the epics) or *'ūd* (Oriental stringed instrument). They used to attend the theatre, especially the plays of Nagīb al-Rīḥanī and al-Kassār. In the good old days, an *ibn al-balad* used to spend not less than a pound per night. In these days a pound meant something, because it would be the equivalent to ten pounds nowadays.

Many interviewees referred to the old days when crafts were outstanding and craftsmen had superior status. In these days they felt they were respected, highly rewarded for their skill, and had self-esteem. This notion about crafts is expressed in the following incident:

> Aḥmad Bahgat, *'usṭā* (expert) in his work, and considered to be the best brass craftsman in Egypt, used to dress in a *galabīyya* and slippers. The British supreme representative sent to Ahmad Bahgat to come and meet him, but Ahmad Bahgat said to the messenger if the supreme representative wants me he should come to me. Hence, the high representative came to our *ḥāra* and requested an *'andīl* (lamp) which took Aḥmed Bahgat a year and a half to finish, and he charged the English supreme representative several hundred pounds.

Although most of the interviewees think that craft life is degenerating and craftsmen are less superior nowadays, some of them still hold on to the old notions of the nature of the crafts, the values attached to them, as well as the superior status a craftsman holds. These notions are expressed in the following words of an old carpenter who is considered by *ahl al-ḥitta* to be a real *ibn al-balad:*

> The craftsman is superior to any other group because the skilled craftsman still gets good clients and good pay. Consequently, he can afford to live comfortably. The craft is a study in the art as well as a study of man. I, for example, have to excel in my craft and in understanding my client. I have to be considerate to my client's status and charge him accordingly. For example, just last week a widow demanded a certain task that cost me three pounds, but I charged her only one and a half; if her husband was alive I would charge her more but he is dead and she is bringing up his orphans. It is my duty to help her.

What is impressive about this carpenter is that he had been one of the best *baladī* carpenters in the *ḥāra* and used to earn a lot of money. But lately because of misfortune he earns so little that he can hardly keep his family alive.

Merchants, like craftsmen, are looked upon as equally superior by the *awlād al-balad.* A textile merchant in the *ḥitta* was referred to in the following terms:

> Ḥāgg Aḥmed al-Humuṣānī, the great merchant in the *ḥitta* and a real *ibn al-balad,* has his house open to anyone, and a lot of people are invited daily to share his meals. He is also very charitable to the poor in a way that is unique for such people. For example, if he notices that someone needs some clothes, he suggests to him that he himself needs some and would like the man to choose it for him. Consequently, the fellow selects something worthy of Ḥāgg Aḥmed. Having done so, Ḥāgg Aḥmed offers it to him as a present.

Besides craftsmen and tradesmen, the butcher and *baladī* coffee shop owners were referred to by all interviewees. "They have to be *awlād al-balad.*" However, *awlād al-balad* were ambiguous when it came to identifying the *futūwa:* If he is good, then the *futūwa* is an *ibn al-balad,* but if he is bad then he is only a thug, i.e. *balṭagī. Awlād al-balad* still retain a specific image of the role of the *futūwa* from the old days. An aging interviewee described the *futūwa* of his *ḥitta* in the following terms:

> Aḥmed Tūma was a manly *futūwa,* i.e. *gad'a*, and a real *ibn al-balad.* He used to dress in a *galabīyya*, had a big mustache and a huge body. His manner was very serious and he never joked or laughed and when he talked he was very precise. He was respected and obeyed by everyone. Any *zaffa* (bride's ceremony) passing in his *ḥitta* had to get his permission and alert him by a special musical tune. On the other hand he was charitable, gallant, and very understanding, well aware of the people's problems and needs.

In wealth the *ibn al-balad* is thought of as a well-to-do working man. However, the strata of *awlād al-balad* from which the typification of *ibn al-balad* has emerged is thought of as mainly the lower classes and in particular the masses. This might seem contradictory but perhaps it can be explained by the changes that have taken place in these quarters. These medieval quarters were earlier inhabited by native Egyptians from a variety of classes, even the upper-classes (as shown in al-Jabartī and Aḥmed Amīn), all possessing a common identity which differentiated them from the rulers and foreigners. Now it seems that only certain lower classes dwell in these quarters and it has been noted by many interviewees that Egyptians who dwell in the medieval quarters leave them when they become rich or educated. Therefore although the social stratification of these quarters has changed, some of the values attached to the previous stratification still persist in the typification of *ibn al-balad.*

In contrast to others' views of them, external features such as attire, speech and mannerisms are not essential elements in the *awlād al-balad's* conception of themselves. However, the important element is that the *ibn al-balad* conceives himself as being something of a dandy, an *'āyi'*, implying cleanliness, tastefulness, neatness and elegance. Even in a *gallābīyya,* he is never shabby or dirty. Ideally, the *gallābīyya* should be of a special type of white linen, *sawakbīs,* accompanied by a special shawl and special shoes. Being dressed in a *gallābīyya* arouses certain feelings in the *awlād al-balad.* For example, one interviewee, regretting that he no longer wears a *gallābīyya* all the time, said:

> Before I used to dress always in a *gallābīyya;* now I am forced to be dressed in a suit, but from time to time I dress in my *baladī-gallābīyya* and when I do so, I feel as if I am in paradise.

Another mentioned that when someone is elegantly dressed it is commonly remarked of him that, "Well, of course nobody is your equal, you are dressed in the *baladī* outfit." Thus to the *awlād al-balad,* it is the manner in which he is dressed that identifies him rather than the dress itself. His manner of speech is also contrary to the popular image portrayed by the actor Muḥammad Riḍā which is rather vulgar and loud. An *ibn al-balad* is supposed to be over-polite in speech and his voice is soft. This conception of the *ibn al-balad* is in line with what Aḥmed Amīn observed some seventy years ago. In his encyclopedia, the term *ibn al-balad* denotes a character with a certain manner of dress and speech as well as a special way of behaving:

> An *ibn al-balad* wears a *gallābīyya,* a robe, a *quftān* and a head-dress *(taqīya),* and gives it particular care. These clothes must fulfill certain conditions. Their material has to be bright, like turquoise blue or pistachio green or vermillion. Its color has to suit the color of the *quftān* and the color of the belt suit them. Shoes have to be a light red, fine leather. He has to be always shaved and his nails cut. On the whole, he should be very careful with every part of his dress. The *jubba* should suit the *quftān* in a symmetrical way and in all this he should be very clean and elegant. As for manners, his voice is very low and he talks slowly and gently and if he walks he has to be careful, if he laughs it has to be quietly, for he has to follow certain rules. If he eats he has to be very elegant and meticulous about the size of the bites he takes and the cleanliness of his fingers as well as his whole attire.

From surveying the significance of various elements in the typification of the *ibn al-balad* one can conclude that most of the elements are not as significant as certain specific personality traits and distinct attributes of the *ibn al-balad.* The *awlād al-balad* emphasized that the significant elements were certain values, namely tradition and custom. It is interesting to note that for the *awlād al-balad* there is an ideal model implied to which they aspire. The remainder of this section will be devoted to analyzing the idealization of the typification of *ibn al-balad.* Idealization in this context refers to what is typical and positive. To *awlād al-balad* the concept implies a glorified past that they wish to reconstruct.

The attribute of virtue symbolizes not only some of the *ibn al-balad's* basic values but also relates to what is conceived of as the ideal *ibn al-balad.*

To *awlād al-balad* the medieval quarters are not slummy and dirty, but rather the original and the traditional Cairo. This was noticed by Nagīb Maḥfūẓ and he expressed it in the following dialogue:

Aḥmad Rashīd speaks:

> This quarter is old Cairo. Its scattered remains arouse sympathy and stir our imagination. But if you look at it logically, you will find nothing except dirtiness. To preserve it you have to sacrifice people. It is worthwhile getting rid of it to give the people a chance to enjoy a happy and healthy life.

Ahmad 'Ākif's answer which pleased the group of *awlād al-balad* who were in the coffee shop was:

> The old is not only dirtiness. It is a memory that can be far superior to any facts of the present. The Cairo that you want to efface is the glorious Fatimid Cairo. How can you ever compare it with the new enslaved Cairo? (Maḥfūẓ 1946 : 54).

It seems that one of the factors which make *awlād al-balad* stick to their quarter is that it is part of their identity. They identify themselves with what is local and old and not foreign. Hence, medieval Cairene quarters confirm their identity. It is as if the quarter had a reality of its own that bestows on them certain values and patterns of behavior.

Inhabitants of medieval Cairene quarters look with contempt upon those who outgrow their own locales; such persons are seen as betraying their origin and values. One informant described how a folk composer who lived in the *ḥitta* became very famous on television broadcasts and everyone in the neighborhood expected him to move to another quarter. This attitude was expressed by everyone in the *ḥitta* and even the children used to call out to him in the streets asking him in a sarcastic way when he was going to leave. When the present writer met him he was very self-conscious and defensive and expressed a sense of guilt. He explained that he had never thought of leaving the quarter and that leaving one's neighbors was, in his opinion, a great offence to his own identity.

This same idea was expressed by Nagīb Maḥfūẓ in the novel *Zuqāq al-Midaq*, with El-Sayyid Raḍwān giving advice to 'Abbās el-Ḥilw when the latter had decided to go and work in the Suez Canal with the English: "Be careful in spending your money, and beware of alcoholic liquor and pork.

Do not forget that you are from the *Midaq* and to the *Midaq* you will return" (Maḥfūz 1963 : 117).

These quarters are not only valued and preserved for their being old but also for their sacredness. In interviewing *awlād al-balad* in al-Ḥusayn quarter one gets the impression that the people there are aware of the sacredness of the place. To them it is full of *baraka* (blessing) and goodness. This is often said in a superior manner: "We are beside al-Ḥusayn." "We are beside the Prophet's house (family)." There is a common feeling in this quarter that, so long as they are beside the Ḥusayn no harm will befall them and that whenever they find themselves in need they can appeal to him. This notion of protection was expressed by Nagīb Maḥfūz in his novel *Khān al-Khalīlī,* when describing the move of Aḥmad 'Ākif's family from 'Abbāssīyya to Khān al-Khalīlī during the bombing of Cairo in the World War II, believing that al-Ḥusayn is capable of protecting the quarter against any bombing. The dialogue between Aḥmad 'Ākif and *al-mu'allim* Nūnū:

> 'Aḥmad 'Ākif: Thank you wise *mu'allim*. It has been often said by the people that the Husayn quarter is safe."
> *Mu'allim* Nūnū: "you believe if and believe it strongly. It is sacred as a quarter and is loved, respected and honored for the sake of its owner. You will see in the coming days that you will not be able to leave it or be separated from it, and a call from within will draw you to it" (Maḥfūz 1965 : 44).

This sacredness of the place not only protects inhabitants from material damages such as bombing but also from immoral behavior. Original settlers of these quarters conceive of themselves as basically moral and religious, hence any immoral behavior would spring from new settlers. They also believe that the saints usually protect them from those people.

To *awlād al-balad,* the simple, beautiful and unsophisticated way of life seems to be correlated with the traditional and local. Being traditional is not only a characteristic of the collectivity but also a value that should be preserved. The *gallābīyya* is not only a local dress but a beautiful one that represents certain traits. For example, when an *ibn al-balad* is forced to dress in a European suit for one reason or another, he always complains of discomfort and the moment he reaches home he changes to a *gallābīyya.* When a person is sitting at a table arranged in the western manner with spoons, forks and knives he is told, "we are all *awlād al-balad* and we can be at ease" meaning that if he wishes to eat with his hands he may do so. *The ṭablīya* (low round table) is not only a local object for food but rather a superior one over a foreign table because it enables them to be more considerate, intimate and aware of their family. As one informant indicated:

> I have a table and I prefer to eat with my children around a *ṭablīya* because this enables me to see every one – to see if any member is

unhappy or taking a lesser portion, not eating or wanting more of anything.

The *baladī* or traditional food is tasty and is usually described as *al-baladī yawkal* (the *baladī* is edible), meaning that what is *baladī* is what is worth eating. Eating with the tips of the fingers is the traditional simple way as well. A person sitting at a table eating in the western manner is often told to eat with his hands if he wishes to do so.

The amount of food cooked is a value in itself because it is considered a measure of how hospitable or important a family is. It goes back to the "good old days" when good families cooked considerable amounts of food daily which went much beyond their needs so that anyone was welcomed to their table at any time. Moreover, a guest was usually received with the additional cooking of a whole sheep. Such a home is often referred to as *bayt maftūḥ*, a term which literally means an open house but it implies hospitality, abundance and status. It is also referred to as *bayt 'ezz* (house of luxury) which, as one respondent who was referring to the importance of his family said, "So much food was consumed in our *bayt 'ezz* daily that a special accountant was there to register the number of birds, sheep, etc." The amount of food is considered important not only because it is an indicator of hospitality and prestige, but also because a person brought up in this kind of home is supposed to acquire certain desirable character traits and attitudes. As one respondent said: "The person brought up in a *bayt 'ezz* is satisfied," which implies that he grows up acquiring integrity, *'afūf*, and is not envious even of the things he cannot have. The logic in this explanation is that the more you have had of something the more you can do without it and this satisfaction extends to things other than mere food. Moreover, the opposite is also true, namely that the less you have the more you want to grab. As a result certain character traits develop such as meanness, greed and envy.

These notions are reflected in certain table manners. For example, when *awlād al-balad* are guests they are very careful not to show a strong desire for food unless their host insists several times. The visitor is expected initially to refuse the food so that he would not be considered greedy and envious and someone from a low house.

Being envious or not satisfied is a charge that *awlād al-balad* would deny strongly by referring to the *'ezz* of the old days. For example, *'umm* Fatḥī, whose neighbors were criticizing her behavior as rather greedy and envious, said in defense: "I have been brought up in *bayt 'ezz* where I have eaten a lot of chickens, pigeons and turkeys, hence though I am very poor now, yet I am satisfied." Another *ibn al-balad* said: "I have to cook a lot of food and insist that my children get a lot, especially the girls, so that when they go to their husband's houses they will already be satisfied."

As with food habits, traditional singing is defined as that which is of intrinsic worth. The preference for traditional singing prevails in these quarters. This preference for local singing is part of their identity; it is often said to persons who claim to prefer foreign songs or music that they are *khawāgāt*, that is, not *awlād al-balad*. This assertion of local identity through songs and music is cleverly exemplified by Nagīb Maḥfuẓ in the following dialogue between *mu'allim* Nūnū and *mu'allim* Zafta on the subject of singing:

> *Mu'allim* Nūnū: Brothers, Muhammad's nation is still all right. Have you ever heard an Englishman – and they have been among us for half a century – singing "Yā layl yā 'ayn"? The truth is that those who prefer foreign singing are like those who long for pork.
>
> *Mu'allim* Zifta: Hear the final word: The best that could be heard is Si 'Abdu if he sings *Yā Layl*, and 'Alī Maḥmūd when he announces the dawn prayer and Um Kulthūm in her song *Fī ummatī al-hawwā*. Any one else is *hashish* mixed with dust (Maḥfūz 1965 : 154).

In talking to *awlād al-balad* one gets the impression that there exist certain customs and shared beliefs to which all levels and strata of the inhabitants of the quarter adhere. For example, *awlād al-balad* visit saints to seek solutions to difficult problems. An informant indicated that in al-Ghūrīyya there is a *shaykh* called Yaḥyā who is a specialist in personal problems. Each Saturday, not less than 300 women visit his tomb for help with problems of marriage, divorce and sterility. Another incident cited by an *ibn al-balad* from the Ḥusayn quarter not only illustrates the influence of saints on their lives, but also shows that such beliefs are shared by the poor as well as the rich. One of the common beliefs among dwellers of al-Ḥusayn is that those who pray the early morning prayer in al-Ḥusayn Mosque forty times will be rewarded by fulfillment of their desires. Among those who kept this habit is al-Hāgg Ḥusayn al-'Āgātī, the owner of the famous Kabab shops in al-Ḥusayn. His wealth, which is estimated by the informant at fifty thousand pounds, is considered a reward for his prayers. Al-Ḥāgg al-'Agātī, in return, expressed his gratitude by sticking to the neighborhood, never having thought of changing his residence.

To *awlād al-balad* the attribute of *shahāma* (gallantry) necessitates being bound by certain moral obligations. Most of the moral obligations that mark a person as having *shahāma* relate to traditional patterns of interaction. The *shahm* person is identified as being *aṣīl* (of good or old stock) meaning that he is very knowledgeable in *al-uṣūl* or traditional etiquette. Such a person will know what is expected of him in each situation and hence fulfill his duty. As an *ibn al-balad* explained it:

> As *awlād al-balad,* if one falls sick in the *ḥāra,* everyone knows his duty towards the sick person; some will offer help at home, others will take over his work responsibilities, while the least anyone will do is to visit him daily to ask about his health and offer him company.

Some of the examples cited as duties in reference to traditional moral obligations are: to be considerate and obedient to your parents, to be considerate toward your neighbors, to respect and obey the old, to be hospitable to visitors, to be loyal and attached to your parents, family, neighbors and your country. For example, it is your duty to help your neighbors and thus you don't wait until they ask your help. It is your duty to offer help without humiliating them. An *ibn al-balad* pointed out that in their neighborhood, when they found one who was in a financial crisis, they tried to help him indirectly. They suggested to him that he circumcise his son thus giving them the chance to offer help in the form of *nuqūṭ* (money gifts) without embarrassing him.

Also in time of death, the bereaved does not do anything. Everybody rushes to help and offer money if needed. One informant indicated that when her son died she did not move from her place and her neighbors and friends were the ones who took over all the ritual; some attended his washing, others followed his coffin to his tomb, buying what was needed and arranging for *shaykhs* to recite the Qur'an as well as taking over the mother's household responsibilities and keeping her company most of the time. Marriages are like funerals, insofar as each is an occasion for sharing and helping. If one person is invited, he invites his friends and these friends invite theirs, and finally the whole neighborhood is attending the festival without invitation. They attend because they believe that it is their duty to share the happiness of their neighbor as well as his responsibilities. One offers a dozen chairs, another arranges for the place, a third sings, some women will dance and some will cook the food or offer the sweets and thus the festival becomes the concern of the whole neighborhood.

To clarify further the meaning of *shahāma* here are three situations which might illustrate the meaning of the word in the everyday life of *ibn al-balad.* These three incidents happened recently in one of the *ḥāra* of Darb al-Aḥmar.

A famous folk artist is referred to as a person who is endowed with real *shahāma.* This artist dwells in the *ḥāra* and his job is to deliver milk to the inhabitants. His income from this job is approximately ten piasters a day, that is three pounds a month. When I met him he was dressed in a *gallābīya* and wooden clogs and since he could not afford to rent a room he was living in the street under the shelter of a few tins and baskets. He had a hobby making statues from gypsum which costs him nothing. A well known journalist came across his works by chance and after examining his statues decided that he was a talented folk artist. He introduced him to the professional art circles. His statues were highly appreciated and he became famous, to the extent that in 1969 a special exhibition was arranged for him. The outcome of the sale of the works came to about one hundred pounds from which he took seventy. Everyone in the district was curious to know what, this homeless and penniless artist would do with the seventy pounds. He did not rent a room, nor did he even buy a new *gallābīyya*; instead he gave the whole sum to his neighbor, who was unemployed and had several children. He considered himself in a much better situation than his neighbor as he had a job and had no children. Therefore, he offered the money to his neighbor so that the latter could buy a hand cart on which to sell macaroni and earn a living. I met him four months after his exhibition which made him famous, he was still living in the street and working as a milk delivery man. But all those I met in the *ḥāra* talked about this incident as an act of *shahāma* that comes only from a real *ibn al-balad*.

The second illustration was cited by a folk composer. He pointed out that since he moved to this *ḥāra* thirty years ago he had not paid a penny for the flat he rented. The owner took no rent because the *shaykh* was blind and his income was limited. Though he has now become a prosperous folk song composer, the owner of the house refuses to take any money from him. The *shaykh* describes this act as one of *shahāma* on the part of the neighborhood. On the other hand, the inhabitants of this *ḥāra* think of the *shaykh* as a genuine *ibn al-balad* who has *shahāma* because he usually volunteers to celebrate any wedding or festival in the neighborhood without taking any money.

The third illustration of *shahāma* was cited by a folk song producer, who lives in the same *ḥāra*. When he was ill in the hospital, almost everyone in the *ḥāra* visited him. One of the neighbors used to come walking from al-Ghūrīyya to the hospital al-Manyal, a distance of about 15 kilometers, because he could not afford the price of the bus-ticket, which is usually a mere one piaster (equivalent of a penny). Not only did he come on foot but on every visit he brought some kind of food as a present, although he could only have paid for it at the expense of his own daily meals.

Associated with the attribute of *shahāma* is that identified by *awlad al-balad* as *gad'anā*. Essentially *gad'a* means "young man." In Cairo fifty years ago the term denoted a specific group called *gad'ān* (plural of *gad'a*) who were known for their excellence in beating and fighting and who specialized in protecting those who sought their help. The police used to fear them, and prison to them was an honour that they could boast of (Aḥmad Amīn p. 134). It is often said now to someone who gets imprisoned, "Prison is for the *gad'ān*," meaning that it is only the strong and the honorable who are imprisoned. As an attribute the term *gad'a* implies manliness and gallantry. *Ibn al-balad* being *gad'a* would not tolerate improper behavior; he would interfere to correct it or at least oppose it. This attitude is well expressed in the saying, "he takes his rights by his own arms." He does not accept injustice or tyranny and usually stands for the weak against the strong. He does not stab his friend in the back or fool him, nor would he strike a person in his own neighborhood, for this would be an improper act of a protector to his guest. *Ibn al-balad* as a *gad'a* always comes through as a man in times of trouble and offers his help.

From the preceeding survey we find that *awlād al-balad* use such terms as *shahāma, gad'ana, futūwa* in their traditional context of meaning. The patterns of behavior and attitudes that emerge from these values are idealized. To them these virtues are the essence of the typification of *ibn al-balad.*

In the following pages, we will try to investigate the *awlād al-balad's* conception of other groups so as to arrive at a better understanding of their self image.

2. Ibn al-Balad's Image of Self in Comparison to Other Strata

The *ibn al-balad* compares himself to men of other Cairene strata, mainly foreigners, the upper classes, the educated middle class, government employees, and rural migrants. Each strata is thought of in terms of a character type: the *khawāga,* the *ibn al-zawāt,* the *effendī* and the *fallāḥ.*

Khawāga

The *khawāga* is the polar type to the *ibn al-balad* who is seen as a real Egyptian. Aḥmed Amīn defines the term *khawāga* as follows:

> In the Egyptian tongue the *khawāga* is a European who is dressed in a suit and a cap whether he is Armenian, Italian, English, or any other European nationality. In Egypt, he is feared and is more honest and educated than the natives (Aḥmed Amīn 1952 : 20).

This attitude of fear and respect towards the *khawāga* might have been more accurate in the past, or among certain sectors of the Egyptian society. Among *awlād al-balad* there is a different conception. The common conception of the *khawāga* among *awlād al-balad* is that he is naive, ignorant of the Egyptian way of life, credulous and easily fooled; he is, moreover, aloof and detached from the native culture, he has never assimilated and has always retained the culture of his origin. *Awlād al-balad* think that the *khawāga* regards himself as of a different, superior stock, looking down with contempt upon the *awlād al-balad* and not wishing to be identified as one of them. They see the *khawāga* as an outsider as well as an intruder; hence, he is in turn viewed as of inferior status while they are superior, since they are the genuine natives of the country.

Ibn al-Zawāt

The most revealing description of the *awlād al-balad* comes from their own conception of the *awlād al-zawāt. Awlād al-balad* think that *awlād al-zawāt* regard them as dirty and look down upon them with contempt and disgust as inferior beings. In so doing, the *awlād al-zawāt* are regarded as negating their Egyptian identity. As one *ibn al-balad* pointed out: "Those who deny their native identity are not worthy of it."

Hence, the *ibn al-balad* identifies the *ibn al-zawāt* as a kind of foreigner. He is a foreigner even in family and business relations. Whereas an *ibn al-balad* is to be trusted because he is a man who keeps his spoken promise, an *ibn al-zawāt* does business with impersonal contracts and bills. It is said, "A man is tied by his tongue," meaning that if he says he will do something he will do it. If one asks an *ibn al-balad* for a hundred pounds, he will give it without a receipt. An *ibn al-balad* who owns a building will rent apartments without a contract. When one of the leasees tries to object, the *ibn al-balad* says, "A man is tied by his tongue." It seems that the *awlād al-balad* have more faith in traditional business procedures than in modern ones. An example of an *ibn al-balad* who followed this to extremes is Ḥāgg Muḥammad al-Fishāwī, the owner of a well-known cafe, "el-Fishāwī", at al-Azhar. He had accumulated great wealth, which he kept at home and when a decree was issued discontinuing the one-hundred-pound currency notes, he changed the LE 140,000 he had in his house into ten-pound currency notes.

To an *ibn al-balad*, the *ibn al-zawāt* is an idle person whose wealth is inherited rather than accumulated by his own effort. He is often described by *awlād al-balad* as:

> someone who inherited his wealth and can do with it whatever he wants. He drives cars, eats freely, and is idle. He is dirty, since he spends unbelievable sums on trivialities. He is usually from a rich family which provides him with his needs. Hence, he depends on his parents' money for living, whereas an *ibn al-balad* depends on his own personal efforts. For example, an *ibn al-balad* starts to earn his living when he is a small boy. In contrast, an *ibn al-zawāt* gets up late and does not leave his house before noon. He spends his time in bars, clubs, or at parties as Westerners do (a loose life is usually identified with Westernization). The *ibn al-balad* is so occupied in earning his daily bread that he rarely has time for leisure or recreation, apart from going to the coffeehouse, or local feasts and special occasions.

The *ibn al-balad* sees himself as a working man, never as a beggar or unemployed, or dependent on anybody. As one proverb puts it "He has to eat from the sweat of his brow." As a working man, he is the sole supporter of his family and thus he does not accept financial help from his wife or anyone. The importance of earning one's own living is expressed in the common saying "Nothing mars a man but the depth of his pocket." This means that any defect may be forgiven a man except that which pertains to the earning of money. If he does not earn his living he is no more a man and hence cannot be an *ibn al-balad.* As for the *ibn al-zawāt,* the *awlād al-balad* see him as "fed by his mother." The fact that they say that he is fed by his mother and not by his father degrades him even more and suggests femininity.

An *ibn al-balad* conceives of the *ibn al-zawāt* as a cowardly, weak, loose person who will not stand up and fight. He is pampered and soft in comparison with the *awlād al-balad.* "He is arrogant and pretentious in dress, manner and actions. He is over-careful about his outer appearance, the way he speaks, the kind of language he uses, etc. An *ibn al-balad* is more outspoken, talks in a relaxed way, is careful and simple and behaves naturally."

To the *awlād al-balad,* the *ibn al-zawāt* is coquettish and effiminate in his manners, which the *awlād al-balad* would call homosexual. Thus, at one of the *awlād al-balad's* intimate gatherings, for example a *ḥashīsh* session, an *ibn al-zawāt* would act naively and would be considered a child among men. He is often referred to by the *awlād al-balad* as *mīmī bey* or one who is mainly concerned with such superficialities as clothes and perfumes. According to one *ibn al-balad,* during times of war the *ibn al-zawāt's* main grief was that imported ties and his favorite perfume were unavailable. Generally, the *ibn al-balad* believes that the class of *awlād al-zawāt* are the source of corruption and immorality in Egyptian society.

Awlād al-balad and *awlād al-zawāt* obviously live in different quarters. The *awlād al-balad* come from traditional quarters, such as Bulāq, while the *awlād al-zawāt* live in the *ifrangī* or foreign quarters such as Zamalek. In these different quarters there exist different types of relationships that emerge from different styles of life.

> In the *baladī* quarters people are keen on keeping up neighborhood ties. Thus a strong sense of concern about neighbors can be observed on the first day a new member joins a *ḥāra.* When he arrives with his furniture, everyone in that *ḥāra* will rush out to help him. You see, an *ibn al-balad,* though poor and struggling hard for a living, is concerned about others, while an *ibn al-zawāt,* who is well off, never cares for those around him.

Another interviewee (a coffee shop owner) referred to this notion of indifference in an incident that happened to him:

> Once I was walking in Garden City and a quarrel started. Immediately I interfered to stop the fight, while to my astonishment the residents of this area did not bother. My friend, who was accompanying me, seeing this indifference of the people, told me not to interfere, but I said to him, "How come? Are we not *awlād al-balad?*" We did not leave the place till I had put an end to the fight.

Yet another interviewee touched upon a further difference between an *ibn al-zawāt* and himself in the following terms:

> An *ibn al-zawāt* eats at an *ifrangī* (foreign) table with a fork and knife, but I eat with my hands at a *ṭablīya.* I have a table but I don't feel comfortable at it and only feel comfortable when I sit with my children and family around the *ṭablīya.* This gathering gives me the chance to observe each one's face, whether happy or sad, and see if everybody has the chance to eat well or not, and if anyone needs more of any kind of food.

The *awlād al-balad* have a notion that those living in *ifrangī* quarters are rather cold, sophisticated, impersonal, calculating and lacking in sociability and helpfulness. A folk poet who lives in an old Cairene quarter summed up this difference in one of his poems:

> The idlers hang out in Zamalek quarter
> And Zamalek quarter is a proper maze.
> Even to think of going there
> Will put your life in danger.
> That's why if you want to describe their life
> You say "our life isn't like that."
> You can see them in the town center
> When a boat-like car passes you by.

The Effendī

As in the case of the *ibn al-zawāt,* an *ibn al-balad's* conception of the *effendī* places each in a different sphere. To most of those who considered themselves *awlād al-balad,* an *effendī* is very much tied down by the routine and discipline of his job. He cares about his job because it is the source of his livelihood. Furthermore, since "his livelihood is in the hands of others," he is not free. Hence, he has to be submissive, diplomatic and even hypocritical to his superiors for the sake of preserving his job. As for the *ibn al-balad,* he lives from day to day. He is restless, adventurous and independent; he is inclined more towards independent and non-government employment. He is either the owner of his own business or works at skilled jobs in private concerns. As was often said, "An *ibn al-balad* likes to be master of himself."

The *ibn al-balad* sees himself as more emancipated and less diplomatic and hypocritical than the white collar worker, and, as the saying goes, "What is in the heart is on his tongue." To the *awlād al-balad,* the bureaucrats are not as virile or as tough as themselves. As one *ibn al-balad* said: "The government employees, or the class of *effendī,* are never called *awlād al-balad.* We would call him 'brat *effendī*' (that is, a mere boy giving himself the airs of men)." To the *awlād al-balad,* the *effendīyya* are effete and women can override them easily.

The bureaucrats, to the *awlād al-balad,* are lower in financial status and hence have different patterns of expenditures. A craftsman compared himself to a bureaucrat as follows:

> I am a leather craftsman and I can do anything, in this craft as well as others. For example, I can work as an electrician and put up lamps and gain three pounds in addition to my work. Hence, we craftsmen are *midardaḥ* and can do any work. I am *arzāqi* (earning my living by the day) and wait for my *riqk.* I work independently and completely on my own. My profit is completely what I earn by my own hands. Usually we craftsmen are much better off than any bureaucrat and what the bureaucrat spends in a month I spend in two days. Not only that, but what I spend in stimulants (tea, coffee, cigarettes, *hashīsh*) amounts to what a bureaucrat gets in a month.

This notion of the *awlād al-balad's* large expenditures as compared to the bureaucrats' was expressed by another interviewee as follows:

> I was drunk one night and I started a fight with some people in the *ḥūta.* I was taken to the police station where the officer started to question me. He asked me 'What is the name of your father?' I answered 'Unknown.' He became outraged and said to me 'You are drunk' and I answered him, 'So what if I am drunk, I drink from my own pocket and what I drink with, you cannot spend on your house the whole month.'

The significance of this remark is that the *awlād al-balad* see themselves not only as earning a lot, but also as spending a lot. In this context they think themselves superior to other strata and especially to bureaucrats. The *awlād al-balad* distinguish themselves from the bureaucrats as well as from people of other quarters on the basis of education. This distinction was expressed by a craftsman in the following terms:

> The highly educated people of Zamalek are certainly different from people here. Those of Zamalek are limited in scope and understanding, unlike the *ibn al-balad* who is *midardaḥ* (alert, active). For example, a person from Zamalek, though he has high degrees, once he starts talking to you, he is incapable of being comprehensible. This is because his knowledge comes from books, not from experience.

This doubt and skepticism about the abilities of the educated *vis-a-vis* the illiterate *ibn al-balad* was stated more explicitly by a folk sculptor in the following way:

> One meets everyday stupid people with certificates who sit at desks and get hundreds of pounds just because they have this piece of paper. Certainly any certificate has its limits, whereas the open mind is unlimited.

This questioning of literacy extends in some cases to an admiration of the ability of some illiterate *awlād al-balad.*

The Fallāḥ

A common image of the *fallāḥ* among the *awlād al-balad* is that his work follows a regular and routine pattern.

> The *fallāḥ*'s day starts at dawn with his going to the fields. He spends the whole day working in the field and by sunset he is back home where he eats and immediately falls asleep. On the other hand, the *ibn al-balad* stays late at night in *baladī* coffee houses, reads newspapers. Even if he is illiterate he listens to the radio or asks the one beside him in the coffee house about the news.

This implies that the *fallāḥ*'s interaction with different people is limited and thus his view of the world is narrow. The *ibn al-balad*, on the other hand, because he lives in the city, interacts with all sorts of people and works at different jobs and hence is much more intelligent than the *fallāḥ*. The *ibn al-balad* is much more at ease in the city than the *fallāḥ* and more carefree; the city is his home. One well-known anecdote tells about the *fallāḥ* who was fooled into thinking that he had bought the Cairo tram system.

The *awlād al-balad* see themselves as not only different from the *fallāḥ* but also superior in status. One *ibn al-balad*, in comparing his standard of living to that of the *fallāḥ*, said:

> The *fallāḥ* can eat anything, sleep anywhere (even with his animals or on the oven). As for the *ibn al-balad*, he is accustomed to a certain clean way of living, even if he is poor. The *fallāḥ* does not mind if he eats *mish* (a very salty cheese) every day, but personally if I eat *mish* one day, I cannot eat it the next day. Also the *fallāḥ* does not see money except seasonally (when he receives cash by selling his crops).

On the other hand, money flows into the hands of an *ibn al-balad* daily, and he spends a lot. What the *fallāḥ* earns per day would not be enough for an *ibn al-balad* to spend on one meal. The *awlād al-balad* see the *fallāḥ* as less experienced and less tactful. Some interviewees mentioned the common saying that when one wants to praise someone's tact he tells him, *"inta zū'"* (you are tactful), or *"inta ibn al-balad."* Another notion of what the *awlād al-balad* mean by urbane or suave is exemplified in the following words of a young interviewee in contrasting himself to a *fallāḥ:*

> A *fallāḥ* in a bus would make everybody hear his dialogue with the lady, whereas I can have her leave the bus and follow me just by a look.

A carpenter in one of the *ḥāras* in describing the difference between the *ibn al-balad*, the *fallāh* and the *ṣa'īdi* (Upper Egyptian) said:

> If a *ṣa'īdi* saw a fight in which his friend is being beaten, he would immediately beat the other fellow blindly. An *ibn al-balad* would investigate first and then fight. The *fallāḥ* would pacify the quarrel

without investigation. A *ṣa'īdi* in his country can kill a person first for the mere reason that his buffalo had eaten some grass from his field. An *ibn al-balad* is strong, but not a fool like the *ṣa'īdi*. Generally in a fight *ibn al-balad* would shout, the *ṣa'īdi* would beat, and the *fallāḥ* would remain quiet.

3. Bint al-Balad's Image of Self and her Comparison to Other Women

As the *ibn al-balad,* the *bint al-balad* compares and contrasts herself mainly to women of three other Cairene strata: upper class, rural migrants and the middle class educated and government employees.

The Fallāḥa

In colloquial parlance *fallāḥa* (female peasant) denotes the very opposite of *bint al-balad,* in terms of both residence and character traits. The *fallāḥa* is regarded as awkward, inept, stupid and narrow-minded. The *bint al-balad* assigns herself to a higher status and shuns certain tasks which a *fallāḥa* would naturally perform, such as carrying on her head a load of pots to be washed in the river. The *fallāḥa's* backwardness is further apparent to the *bint al-balad* in a crudeness of taste in furnishings, clothing and hair style. The synonym for crude taste is, in fact, *fallāḥī.* (However, upper-class Egyptian women regard things ructis or in poor taste as "*baladī*".)

An important point of contrast between the *bint al-balad* and the *fallāḥa* concerns cleanliness. This is well illustrated by the remark of one *bint al-balad* who said, "The *fallāḥa* may become modernized and wear flowery and chic dresses, but underneath you will find total filth, whereas the *bint al-balad* is particularly clean both inside and outside." Bodily cleanliness for the *bint al-balad* involves removing all bodily hair, a procedure called *al-ḥifūf,* performed either in a public bath or at home. Cleanliness is also manifested in the care given to the female organs: after intercourse, the *bint al-balad* will wash herself thoroughly.

Cleanliness, however, is not related to hygiene alone. A *bint al-balad* is concerned that she appear glamorous (*'ay'a, ghandūra*). Her "sex appeal" lies in exaggeratedly large eyes, fine features, a round, lively face, and a cameleon body that is well rounded, and not fleshy or boney. The glamorous effect, however, must be maintained with a certain reserve and modesty. Both glamor and modesty are combined in the *bint al-balad*'s outdoor wearing apparel, the *milāya laff,* which reveals the graceful bodily curves yet will "cover" (*tustur*)[1] figuratively what should not be revealed or what is shameful.

---

[1] *Tustur* literally means "covers". By extension it applies also to those who (being *mastur*) are neither poor nor rich but have just enough to keep themselves

Conservative modesty is an attribute which a *bint al-balad* and a *fallāḥa* share. But the *bint al-balad* perceives her rural sister as more modest than herself because she is less modern. In turn, the *fallāḥa* refers to *banāt al-balad* as *gaziyya* (gypsy) because in the house she wears open and sleeveless dresses which the *fallāḥa* would not wear.

The *bint al-balad* regards the *fallāḥa* as bumbling, awkward, slow, unaware of tact and inarticulate. In contrast, she sees herself as *ḥidi'a* (clever), implying a rapid intuitive grasp of any situation, or, as the common saying has it, "one who understands what is still in the air." One can take advantage of the *fallāḥa* and can make a fool of her, but not so with the *bint al-balad,* who is more likely to be the one fooling others. A popular description of *bint al-balad* is one who "is capable of playing with an egg and a stone at the same time" – without breaking the egg. She sees herself as alert and enquiring – attributes emanating from a style of life that brings her into contact with a wide variety of people and situations. It was inconceivable to *mu'allima* 'Azīza that one *fallāḥa*, a resident of the quarter for thirty years, did not know how to go alone to the next *ḥitta.* In comparison to the *fallāḥa*, the *bint al-balad* is *mitfanaṭa*,[2] experienced; *fahlawīyya*, able to interact with anyone with quickness and confidence; and *midardaḥā*, open and alert.

Upper class women (Banāt al-Zawāt)

Bint al-balad also contrasts herself to *banat al-zawāt* (upper class "aristocratic" women). *Banāt al-zawāt* are regarded as "the high gentry of Garden City and Zamalik," remote from and elevated above the *banāt al-balad.* They act like Europeans and are ultra-modern in material possessions, attitudes, and customs. Basically, however, *bint al-balad* views her aristocratic counterpart as one who wears an elegant exterior to cloak an immoral self "of which only God is aware." *Bint al-zawāt* is seen as spoiled and lazy, attending only to her personal appearance and shunning daily family and housework. *Bint al-balad,* on the other hand, would sacrifice all for her

independent of others' support. Thus a common invocation is *"Allāhu yusturak"*, May God enrich you so that you need not seek the help of others and thus be forced to humiliate yourself by revealing personal affairs and secrets. In the same context is the expression *"Rabbina yustur 'ardik"*, an invocation made for an unmarried girl for God to provide a husband to protect her honor and reputation.

[2] The term *mitfanaṭa* literally means "classified." In colloquial Egyptian, the term means to classify things, to put things in order, of things so varied that they seem to be disordered. Hence, as an attribute, *mitfanaṭa* implies the latter aspect, of variation and disorder. To *baladī* people, *mitfanaṭa* describes how they see themselves as experienced and therefore unable to be fooled.

husband's and family's welfare and sees herself as superior as a wife and mother.

Bint al-zawāt's aloofness and sophistication lead her to refrain from many activities and habits which *bint al-balad* would consider natural. For example, *bint al-balad* would "not hesitate to scold and beat anyone who annoys me. I do not feel shy about sitting on the ground or in a *baladī* coffee-house if I am tired, whereas *bint al-zawāt* would never have the guts to do so." The *bint al-balad* sees herself as courageous and outspoken in words and actions. As a *baladī* woman, it is natural to eat with one's hands, to wear the *milāya-laff*, and to use traditional utensils. *Mu'allima* Bahiya described one family as "high" because of "their adherence to a specified weekly menu and their use of knives and forks."

Intimate and personal ties are highly valued by the *bint al-balad*. The remoteness of the *bint al-zawāt* makes her appear unsympathetic, impersonal, and selfish in her neighborly relations. *Umm* Fatḥī's experience of the *ḥitta* exemplifies this:

> Garden City may give you peace and quiet but never the sociability and considerateness you find here, on all occasions, in joy or misfortune. If I say "ah" in pain, everyone around rushes to help me; someone knowledgeable in *baladī* remedies prescribes one and another volunteers to fetch a doctor. Can you find this spirit in Garden City?

Bint al-balad's sense of identity is more strongly linked to her quarter (*ḥitta*) than to members of the nuclear or extended family. *Bint al-zawāt*, however, identifies herself with such-and-such *Bey* or *Pasha*[3] – the most prominent male member of her family. For *bint al-balad*, to leave her quarter is to negate her identity and her origin. For this she would be mocked and accused of trying to put on the airs of an aristocratic lady.

Educated women

Bint al-balad not only differentiates herself from but considers herself equal in knowledge to the educated woman, since the "school of life" exceeds any formal training. In adhering to certain values and standards of behavior, *bint al-balad* is even superior. *Mu'allima* 'Azīza tells of an "educated" niece who had illicit relations with a man. "This girl cared for neither honor nor reputation; she is worthless. This is something a *bint al-balad* would never have allowed." *Umm* Bulbul cites the example of a famous doctor who married an educated woman, and regrets he had not married a *bint al-balad* who would have "comforted him and made him feel a man. His

---

[3] *Bey* and *Pasha*, Turkish titles that denote high status and prestige, i.e., wealthy families.

'educated' wife criticizes his behavior and objects to his many personal demands."

To the *banāt al-balad,* an educated woman becomes snobbish, looking down on the *ḥitta* and desiring to leave it at once. *Umm* Ga'far's brother married an educated woman who refused to receive his family at the wedding because they were *baladī*-dressed women. "This woman should realize that we, *banāt al-balad,* brought up her husband, educated him, and made him a man." However, if an educated woman does not negate her identity as a *bint al-balad* she is respected as genuine. As one *bint al-balad* observed:

> My neighbor's mother works as a ward attendant in a hospital but she herself is university-educated and works as an airline hostess. She married a doctor but still lives in the *ḥitta.* She loves *baladī* people, talks like them, and follows their style of life. Occassionally she holds a *zār* and invites us. She is a real *bint al-balad.*

Nevertheless, despite some feelings of superiority to the educated woman, the *bint al-balad* aspires to an education and regards it as an improvement on instinctive knowledge. She may feel inferior to her educated daughter, and yet want her to have a school education. One often hears, "learning is as important as religion. However *mitfanaṭa* (experienced) I am, there will be things I do not know that an educated girl will know."

As a working woman, the *bint al-balad* is a *bint al-sūq* ("daughter of the market") which implies a character-type associated with the nature of the job – buying and selling fruits, vegetables, butter, fish, etc. *Mu'allima* Zuhra, as a *bint al-sūq*, is exposed to all kinds of people and experiences and observes many kinds of human problems. Such work requires foresight and intelligence; it is said, "one *bint al-balad* equals twenty men in trading." In contrast, a woman employee in the government is "bound to her desk and hence lacks experience and is unaware of the world about her." Thus, *bint al-sūq* denotes cleverness and a certain worldly poise or ease in any economic or social situation. For example, women clients come to *Mu'allima* 'Azīza in her butcher shop with a variety of complaints: difficulty in finding servants, bad treatment from their husbands, financial problems, etc. "The market is life and this is our school," 'Azīza remarked. The marketplace provides contact with a wide range of behavior and social problems, thereby enriching the *bint al-sūq*'s own experience in comparison to the woman confined to her home.

Serveral women of the *ḥitta* do governmental work. The *bint al-balad* regards the salaries they make as too low to make it worthwhile to neglect the home. Zaynab, for example, earns eighteen Egyptian pounds per month and her husband is in debt. But Zaynab neglects her husband and thinks only of her personal appearance and pleasures. The *bint al-balad* considers the government employee conceited, superficial, and neglectful of her wifely duties. This explains why she spends her salary only on selfish, superficial pleasures.

The Opposite Sex

Bint al-balad's relation to the opposite sex is governed by certain values that color her behavior and hence reflect her self-concept. She conceives of herself as honorable and modest. The *milāya-laff* is a suitable dress for her because it protects her modesty, just as a mini-skirt would injure her modesty. One *bint al-balad* recounted the time a woman, not originally from the *ḥitta*, came wearing a mini-skirt. "Everyone ridiculed her and one of the *ḥitta* grabbed her handbag and threw it on the ground. When she bent down to pick it up everything showed and everyone regarded her with contempt until the holy blessing of the saints rid the *ḥitta* of her." The emphasis on modesty is often due to the *ḥitta*'s being considered a sacred place, owing to the location of tombs of saints (*awlīyā*) in it. Indecency is therefore an offence. One *bint al-balad* observed that "the saints' tombs of the quarter protect us from immodest and dishonorable people and drive them away."

Concern for reputation is another aspect of this conservatism. Women of the *ḥitta* are known by all and their actions are closely observed. Their behavior must accord with the *ḥitta*'s expectations of them. Even a youngster is allowed to reprimand immodest behavior. An unmarried woman's reputation can be ruined by the mere rumor of her going around with a man before marriage. This could stigmatize her, or "break her wings" as one phrased it, leaving her without pride. In such a state people regard her as corrupted (in the village she might be shot). Hence, the *bint al-balad* does not appear in the streets with a man who is not her father, brother, or uncle. Intimate gestures between unmarried couples are scorned. One *bint al-balad* recounted the following:

> "One day I met my nephew in the street. He lives in another area and is not known in our neighborhood. Because he is unable to speak, he has the habit of holding one's hand while communicating. While I was talking to him in this manner, a man from the *ḥitta* stopped me and took me home. This suspicion was not lifted until my mother confirmed my story."

Walking hand-in-hand with a man who is known to be the *bint al-balad's* fiancé is not proper as long as no official contract has been made between them. One *bint al-balad* who owns a shop in the neighborhood was complaining that her relative goes hand-in-hand with her fiancé (and they have been rumored to be lovers), although they have not even been formally engaged: "I have been in the *ḥitta* for twenty-five years and I have netted this shop one thousand pounds. Yet I am going to sell the shop and leave the *ḥitta* because of the disgraceful behavior of my relative."

Nor should a girl be photographed with a man who is not a close relative. A man from the *ḥitta* (and a university graduate) narrated this incident: "I wanted to propose to a neighbor of mine of whom I was very fond. But I changed my mind when I saw a photo of her and a male neighbor. I wouldn't permit my sister to do this, and I would expect my fiancée to be similarly conservative."

Receiving men at home in the absence of the father or husband is considered very improper, and numerous stories are cited to show how this behavior may have harmful consequences. An elderly *bint al-balad* used to leave her daughter with a male teacher in the house for private lessons. After a few months, he became fond of the girl and had sexual relations with her. "The greatest blame falls on the mother who allowed a stranger in the house and then left him alone with her daughter." The man was considered vile and low, but he was excused on the basis that "you cannot have petrol and matches near each other and at the same time not expect fire." The girl too was blamed, and it was felt she was not a real *bint al-balad,* or else she would have protected her honor. The main issue in this case was that the girl allowed premarital sexual relations – the most shameful and condemned act in these quarters – and the only thing that saved her from being completely ostracized was that the man proposed to her.

When a man proposes to a woman in such a situation, neither *mahr* (dowry) nor *shabka* (betrothal gift) are expected of him. This is very humiliating to the bride since the *mahr* and *shabka* are very important to *banāt al-balad.* For *banāt al-balad* not only boast of the amount paid to them, they also take great pride in the speed with which the money is paid. One well-to-do woman prided herself upon the fact that her daughter's suitor was ready to pay 300 pounds immediately and wanted to marry her within the month. Such an attitude on the part of the suitor reflects the girl's great desirability as well as the fact that he is well off and is ready to "buy" her. "Buy" in this context refers to nonmaterial aspects since the amount of *mahr* symbolizes the girl's status in terms of family, personal reputation, and beauty. *Banāt al-balad* are thus always urged to choose, as the common saying goes, "he who desires you, not the one whom you desire."

The *bint al-balad* is assumed to be honorable and capable of protecting herself. She is described as "one who can be trusted among a hundred men" and "she is a man among men and no one can fool her." When a young *bint al-balad* expressed her fear of men molesting her in the street, the immediate reaction of the men present was, "Do you really fear men in the street? I am sure that if any man dares to bother you, you would immediately take off your shoe and beat him."

Flirting is a frequent kind of interaction between sexes in the *ḥitta.* "A man keeps following *bint al-balad,* thinking he is cute. When he finds that she is not interested in him, he becomes irritated and insults her, saying, 'Who do you think you are?' and he pretends that it is she who was accosting him." On the other hand, the *bint al-balad* who is careful about her reputation realizes that such talk could ruin her. If she is courageous and outspoken, she will finally beat him physically, since she know that a strong reaction is expected of her to preserve her reputation. The following is an incident recounted by a 20-year-old *bint al-balad:*

> A certain cowardly *ḥashīsh* merchant persisted in flirting with me several times. He even followed me to the movie and sent me tea with the waiter in the movie. The fact that I rejected his advances prodded him into saying dirty things about me in the quarter, like "loose woman" and "daughter of a whore." One day I became furious and followed him to the *baladī* coffee house, snatched off his glasses, and beat him with my shoe. He tried to insult me again, but I answered back with a flood of insults. He even took a chair and tried to hit me with it, but I ducked and he fell and I fell on him and beat him. On that day I shocked the market; everybody heard about this incident, particularly since this man was known and feared as a tough guy. Since that day he has lost the respect of others. Had I not done what I did, he would have kept on saying I am a loosewoman.

By beating him she not only put a stop to his improper behavior and protected her reputation, but she also humiliated him so badly that he had to leave the neighborhood. He would never again be considered manly and would be constantly reminded, "You have been beaten by a female. You are not a man."

This does not mean that flirting is always rejected. On the contrary, it is often used as a means of getting acquainted. As one man pointed out, *"Bint al-balad* at first refuses flirtation and may hit the flirt with her slipper. But it may end with understanding and harmony between them." Since molesting may ruin a woman's reputation it must be done in a very subtle way if it is to achieve harmony. For example, the *bint al-balad* will walk with one of her friends and the would-be flirt will walk with one of his. The two men start talking in a voice loud enough for the courted girl to hear. The conversation seems to be taking place between the two men; however, their words are really addressed to the girl. She is made aware of this by the two-fold implication in their choice of words. The girl answers by talking to her friend in similar terms. The conversation between the interested couple is far from obvious to the outsider. Such dialogue relies on puns, cleverly-chosen words, and jokes in which the hero is the suitor.

The Husband

Bint al-balad's concept of her husband reflects her concept of herself as woman and wife. To *bint al-balad,* the support of the family (including her own support) is the full responsibility of the husband and is part of his identity as a man. A man should be capable of "feeding his wife." This expression is used symbolically to denote his ability to earn money to provide for his family. The husband who does not fulfill this role is described as "one who is fed by his wife." He is not a man and is often called a "female" (*mara*), which is a most degrading status for a husband.

The ideal husband in the *bint al-balad's* eyes is a well-to-do man who enables his wife to be a "lady" (*sitt*), a nonworking woman who has the leisure to sleep as long as she likes, servants for the housework, and all the comforts and luxuries she desires. Thus what is important is not only the fact that she does not have to work to earn her living, but also that her husband can afford the luxury of maintaining her in style. It is interesting to note that though *bint al-balad* claims to disdain certain attitudes of upper class women, she still aspires to the same material comforts which those women enjoy, wishes that her husband might provide them, and to some degree idealizes that situation.

Bint al-balad expects men to prefer a housewife to a working woman. One educated man indicated that men are now seeking working women as wives in order to raise the family income, but a woman responded, "it might be true that men now desire working women as partners, because of the rise in the cost of living, but deep in their hearts they prefer a housewife if they are real men." It is expected that the husband of a *bint al-balad* who worked before marriage will demand that she leave her job, if he wishes to assert his identity as a man who does not need the financial help of his wife. An elderly *bint al-balad* pointed out that her two daughters, who were government employees when they got married, were asked by their husbands to resign. The girls did not object; "after all, their husbands are well off."

Husbands who insist that their wives work are looked down upon. One *bint al-balad* complained: "My husband, who is married to two other women, is treating me badly because I don't 'bring him money' as do the other two women." She was objecting because her salary would go into his personal pocket when he should be the one to provide for the whole family.

If she wishes to work, *bint al-balad* considers her income a supplement to her husband's, to be used as she wishes, with no obligation toward her husband or the household expenditures. But if her income should be needed for househould provisions, she will be the first one to sacrifice her personal desires. A man commented, "The income of the wife is for herself; it should not be spent on the husband. He is the one who should feed her." Men who have no occupation in these quarters are referred to disdainfully as "those who are fed by their mothers." If, on the other hand, the woman happens to spend her income on the family either because of some shortage in the husband's income or for some other reason, she thereby acquires a higher status. One *bint al-balad* remarked that "any woman who has authority over her husband is usually one who has an income and provides for her home."

Some *banāt al-balad* (especially elderly ones) prefer a man of the quarter (*ibn al-balad*) to a government employee. "How could anyone prefer an *effendī* over an *ibn al-balad*, when the *effendī's* pocket is always empty and the *ibn al-balad's* is always full?" "The *effendī* will never be preferred to the *ibn al-balad* because his income is limited. Once he is done with the butcher and grocer, nothing is left of this salary."

But it is not wealth as much as the ability to earn one's own living that is at the core of *bint al-balad's* notion of masculinity. One young *bint al-balad* noted that some girls prefer *ḥashīsh* merchants (who are rich) as husbands. The common reaction of elderly women was: "Those who prefer *ḥashīsh* merchants are the ones who come from a similar environment." To *banāt al-balad* a real *ibn al-balad* and an ideal husband "is a man who earns his living from the sweat of his brow."

As a "real man," the husband should know and fulfill his obligations. The husband's main duty is meeting the needs of his home. Many *banāt al-balad* express their appreciation of their husbands in the following terms: "What a man! He fulfills my every wish, he keeps my home full of everything and showers me with jewels." The husband who can afford jewelry provides his wife with far more than her immediate needs. Jewelry, especially gold, is not so much an ornament as an investment and a sign of prestige. A woman with high prestige is said to be "dressed in jewelry up to her elbows." The value of gold is stable, and when a woman buys jewelry it is usually thought of as "an asset to help in time of crisis." Thus, while the ideal husband would add to her jewelry, a bad husband would force her to sell it. As they say, "he disarmed me of the jewelry that I was keeping for a time of need."

The husband should also control his home. For *banāt al-balad* control of the home means that "he knows everything within it. For example, he knows the price of a cup of tea as well as the price of a meal, and he brings the provisions himself." If the husband neglects these activities and the wife takes over, he loses her respect. For example, *Umm* Faṭhī's husband used to work as a tailor but because of his *ḥashish* addiction he started to neglect his work and home responsibilities to the extent that she had to take over. "I had to buy even his *gallābīyya* for him because I had to make him appear respectable in front of people. But he became so irresponsible in his life and his home that we had to separate. He is not a 'homely man;' he is a *ḥashīsh* addict, mean and vile."

The husband is also expected to control his wife. To control her means being aware of all her activities, knowing when she goes out and comes back, where she goes and whom she meets. He has to be tough, that is, "a lion," otherwise his wife will have no regard for him. The relationship between the husband's masculinity and his control over his wife is made clear in the following: *Mu'allīma* 'Azīza, the butcher, said, "My sister, who is a *bint al-sūq*, married a man who is soft. She started to lead her own life and became a 'sport,' that is, she came and went at her leisure. Whenever her husband dared to object she would kick him out of the house. Finally she had to leave him to marry a real man." Another working *bint al-balad* cited the incident of a woman married to a man who was weak but who provided her with a luxurious life. For a long time this woman carried on an affair with another man until it was discovered by chance, when she and the man were in a car accident. The *bint al-balad* commented on that incident: "As long as the husband is soft, the woman will do what she wants. Unless he is like a 'lion,' the woman will neither fear nor respect him. If the woman gets spoiled it is due to the man; if she stays pure it is also due to him."

The husband who does not control his home and wife is not respected; he is not considered a real man, for his wife overrules him. A real man may be so tough that he beats her, but *banāt al-balad* are of the opinion that a beating is nothing but an expression of jealousy that springs from love, and they appear not to mind greatly their husband's beatings. "A beating from one's love is as sweet as eating raisins." Since it is also an expression of the masculinity and toughness that are expected of the husband, there is nothing really shameful in being beaten.

The emphasis of *bint al-balad* on the virility of her husband springs not only from the importance of intercourse to her but also from the status she derives from being the object of sexual attention. One elderly *bint al-balad* explains: "The woman who agrees to live with an impotent man deserves the consequences of this choice, because in this case she should become a servant. The free woman would ask for divorce." It is the duty of a virile husband to satisfy the woman in sexual relations by having frequent and lengthy intercourse.

Three *banāt al-balad* debated the importance of the husband's virility. *Umm* Fardūs was divorced from her husband for two years because he married a young girl. She and her husband agreed to remarry on condition that he keep his young wife. When they had remarried, he rented a separate apartment for her and agreed to provide fully for her and for his children. He visited her every now and then, but *umm* Fardus complained that he did not sleep with her. The second women said to her that as long as he looked after her and the children and fulfilled her needs, why the complaint? *Umm* Fardūs' immediate reaction was:

> How could you say that? This is not even accepted by the Islamic *sharī'a*. Life is not only food and drink: we are human beings who need other things too. The wife certainly needs a man who will sleep with her. What will she feel when she sees the husbands of her women neighbors coming back to them at the end of the day to sleep in their arms? Of course she will be jealous and boil with frustration.

The third woman said, "Why have marriage then, if it were just a matter of food and drink or money? I had them in my father's home, anyway. What I need is a man in my lap."

Bint al-balad conceives of herself mainly as a housewife who has certain duties to fulfill toward her home, husband, and children. Her main duty toward her husband is to make life comfortable for him, that is, "prepare his bath, dress him, cook for him, clean and take care of the home, and please him." These duties are expected of her regardless of whether she is only a housewife or a working woman as well. A working *bint al-balad* said: "We *banāt al-sūq* have to free ourselves on certain days for our men. Otherwise, if I am busy all the time, he will wonder why he married me. I have to change dresses for him because if he always sees me working and busy and tired, he will say (and he would be right) why didn't you stay unmarried?" She is careful to dress and to groom herself every night, to appear at her best when he comes home, as an expression of her interest in pleasing him, all of which are part of her conception of her role as a wife.

She also sees herself as an efficient housekeeper, capable of living on the smallest of incomes, which contributes to the establishment of her husband's career. It is often said about men who have accumulated wealth that it was due to the cleverness of their wives. *Umm* Ḥasan, who married a worker, uncomplainingly helped him by working from early morning till late at night to provide for her home, her husband, and five children. She continued to do so until her children had grown up and her husband was able to buy his own shop. Everyone said she was an example of a real *bint al-balad,* the "one who lives," meaning that she tolerates any standard of living without complaining, for the sake of her husband, her children, and her home.

Therefore, whether she is a working woman or housewife, her main concern is her family; when her husband can afford to provide her with the needs of life, she doesn't work. Conditions are changing and increasingly the women of these quarters will have little choice: poverty dictates that they must work, as well as to continue to look after their families. Their images of others will undoubtedly change, albeit slowly, in response to the changing conditions.

CONCLUSION

In surveying the usage of the term *awlād al-balad* we can conclude that the term implies a specific collectivity. To attempt to place this collectivity in the social stratification system of Cairo along the lines of horizontal (class) divisions or in terms of mosaic pattern or vertical segments is rather difficult. This is partly due to the complexity of Egyptian society and partly due to the inadequacy in such contexts of analytical tools such as "class," "segments" and "mosaic."

Prior to the twentieth century, one could distinguish two broad social categories in Egypt: *awlād al-balad* and non *awlād al-balad,* underlying the complexity of the society. Each category had its own internal systems of stratification as well as a degree of self-consciousness in relation to outsiders.

At that time, the foreignness of the non *awlād al-balad* was not only based on ethnic differentiation, language, and culture but also on the degree of exploitation and lack of identification with the majority of the indigenous population. The ruling group constituted one section of foreigners. Their foreignness was further emphasized by their control of the coercive apparatus and their power of exploitation. Though Muslims, they were exclusively Turco-Circassian in origin, language and self-identity. Despite their ethnic background and their small numbers they occupied the major offices of the state which gave them access to sources of economic wealth. Their power was imposed upon the local population from whom they remained aloof.

For the early part of the nineteenth century there are several estimates of the size of the Turkish population. Lane estimated their number at 10,000 at a time when the whole population was less than two million. Although estimates vary, none exceeds a figure of 40,000 out of a total population of approximately three million. To the Turkish elite, *awlād al-balad* were *fallāḥīn* i.e. inferior in status. For example, Taher Pasha the *Wālī*, when informed of his deposition, said: "I am appointed by the Sultan and I will not be deposed by the *fallāḥīn*" (al-Jabartī: 626). The ruling group, which conceived of themselves as of stock superior to the local population, were keen to keep it pure by not assimilating with the indigenous population. Their foreignness was intensified by their keeping the Turkish language and by maintaining their numbers through continuous replenishment from the outside. Even the upper strata of *awlād al-balad* who had achieved power and status and at some point worked closely with the governing elite were never accepted by them as equal partners.

In that sense, the other Muslim ethnic groups, i.e. Yemenites, Sudanese, North Africans and Syrians, were obviously less foreign and had the potential to be assimilated with the indigenous population. They shared religion and language with *awlād al-balad* as well as the inferior subject status that made them the target of the same discriminating measures from the governing elite. The Copts, who certainly shared the inferior status of *awlād al-balad*, became alienated from the indigenous population by identifying with the governing body, especially in times of crisis. At the same time, the Western foreigners in Egypt prior to the nineteenth century were a marginal group. Their role in the society was limited, compared to the Turco-Circassian group. They did not occupy major offices of state nor accumulate enough wealth to control the indigenous population. Rather, they lived isolated in their quarters but with no sense of superiority. On the other hand *awlād al-balad* seem to have had no feeling of inferiority in interacting with them.

The indigenousness and homogeneity of *awlād al-balad* emerged not only from a common origin, culture and religion, but also from a common subordinate position and a common struggle *vis-a-vis* a foreign ruling group. The indigenous population of Cairo, though subordinate in status to the foreign elite, nevertheless enjoyed a position higher than the peasant population. Those who achieved the highest status were mainly the upper strata of the *'ulamā'* and merchants. Although wealthy and powerful, *'ulamā'* and merchants did not always ally themselves with the foreign elite; some *'ulamā'* acted as leaders of the rest of the indigenous population. There were various organized links between the *'ulamā'*, acting as guardians of religion and interpreters of the *Sharī'a*, and the masses. As leaders they were not alienated from the masses. On the other hand the masses within the popular quarters were organized under the informal leadership of their *futūwa* (*zu'r, shuṭṭār, 'usab, 'uyyāq* and *kabīr*). These two levels of informal leadership (that is, the *'ulamā'* and the *futūwa*), usually collaborated to restrain excesses of the foreign ruling elite.

But it seems that even the group occupying the lowest ranks among the indigenous population, though labelled in pejorative terms, would still conceive of themselves as *awlād al-balad.* They comprised, after all, the bulk of the indigenous urban population. There is no evidence that they saw themselves as inferior to other groups in the society. On the contrary, there are hints of their sense of superiority, especially as followers of Orthodox Islamic tradition.

The most pejorative labels (and hence the lowest in status) were *zu'r, shuṭṭār, 'uyyāq* and *'usab*, regarded by the ruling elite as outlaws, but conceived of by themselves as heroes. The previous labels are used in early epic literature differently reflecting the self image of the groups. The traits of craftiness, cleverness and a sense of humor stem not from classic Arab values but seem rather to be an Egyptian overlay. The combination of the Arab values and the Egyptian is unique to the *siyar* of the Egyptian heroes. For example, from childhood 'Alī al-Zaybak al-Miṣrī (a folk hero) would not allow anybody to degrade or abuse him. He was brave, courageous and generous. He was also cunning and was known for the tricks he played on his teachers to get what he wanted. As a grown man he became a well-known hero who revolted against the rulers of different Muslim dynasties, but his primary loyalty to the Muslim Caliph (God's representative on earth) was unquestioned. His tools for overcoming his opponents were not only courage and strength but also craftiness, cleverness and intelligence.

We find, therefore, that the urban masses, including the wealthy strata of the indigenous population, distinguished themselves from all foreigners by appropriating to themselves the identity of *awlād al-balad.* In return, the foreign elite referred pejoratively to the masses as animals (*al-awbāsh*) or rabble (*ghawghā'*) and to their leaders as outlaws (*alzu'r, al-shuṭṭār, 'uyyāq*). Historians have referred to the Cairene popular movements as directionless and chaotic, but the very participants in these upheavals identified themselves, in folk tales and ballads, as heroes, capable of changing rulers and of avenging those who suffered injustice. Indeed, these movements were not simply chaotic, since by acts of violence, sabotage and rioting (or even by passive resistance) they did achieve some limited success in minimizing the abuses and exploitation of the authorities. Cairo's popular rebellions belong more properly to the classic archaic, pre-political urban movements described by Hobsbawm:

> The mob may be defined as the movements of all classes of the urban poor for the achievement of economic or political changes by direct action – that is, by riot or rebellion – but as a movement which was as yet inspired by *no specific ideology;* or, if it found expression for its aspiration at all, in terms of traditionalism and conservatism (Hobsbawm 1971 : 110).

Although the Cairo mob had no lasting ideological allegiance it was nevertheless capable of mobilizing behind leaders who were reformists, such as the religious leaders (*'ulamā'*). Even then, though they might be capable of changing a ruler, they did not seek to alter the political or social order. Moreover, from the time of Muḥammad 'Alī (1805–1849) on, historical sources are silent as to the participation of the *futūwa* in revolts or movements until the much later uprising of 1919. Rather there are indications of individual patriotic acts, perhaps a reflection of a strongly centralized government after 1882, coupled with the systematic effort after 1919 to disarm all self-appointed leaders.

Therefore, it can be argued that by the turn of the nineteenth century, the concept of *ibn al-balad* referred to a homogenous, prestigious entity that had an effective role *vis-a-vis* the ruling elite. The intensity of group identity, and the size of any such group, depended on who was opposing or intruding on these indigenous groups. This phenomenon usually reached its peak during Western campaigns.

Contrary to what took place in earlier centuries, in the nineteenth century and in the twentieth century there was a European foreign ruling elite which was not opposed by a homogenous indigenous entity. Foreignness was no longer an attribute only of actual foreign groups but also of certain attitudes, values and life styles within various segments of the indigenous population itself. Westernization of part of this indigenous population eradicated that homogeneity and broke the cultural entity into segments. Thus western education, fashions, and life styles became means and symbols of status and progress. In general, it was the Egyptian elite who first had access to these means. But gradually, with the growth of economic, intellectual and cultural domination, increasing segments of the indigenous population acquired these means. The consequences of this process not only created a social gap between these segments and *awlād al-balad*, but also caused a decline in the latter's effectiveness and a shrinking of their status though they were numerically increasing.

Rapid increase of population and the equally increasing poverty made the westernized segment of the society a numerically thin layer of upper and middle classes at the top. The new middle and upper classes, which emerged mainly from the group of *awlād al-balad* of the eighteenth and nineteenth centuries, were trying to negate that identity and relate themselves to a completely western frame of reference. They also were attempting to lead the whole society and change it according to their modern conceptions. The rest of the population, particularly the urban masses, though poor, powerless and deprived of a meaningful leadership (that stemmed from it and even worked for its interests), retreated and became isolated in its own identity.

Hence, prior to the 1952 revolution, we see that there was a complete dichotomy within Egyptian social structure. The polarity that existed in the eighteenth and nineteenth centuries between foreigners and the indigenous population emerged within the latter. Thus, within the indigenous group there emerged two polar entities. One (the upper westernized classes) had uprooted itself completely from its past, that is, its *awlād al-balad* identity. The other (the masses) became isolated within that same identity. The consequence was an obvious discontinuity between the past and present of certain segments of the society (upper and middle classes) and a retention of the masses to a glorified past. The gap between the two entities was striking.

After the 1952 Revolution the gap between the two began to narrow, and the aspiration for a more authentic identity emerging from one of local origins began to make itself felt. It became quickly apparent, however, that the gap was bridged between the two only at the ideological level of socialist slogans. At the level of societal interaction the gap remained, and the same process of alienation of the masses continued as before. That is, once certain segments of the indigenous population had access to status and power they sought to emulate European models of "success." This, however, placed them on the horns of a dilemma, for at the same time they sought to recapture a deeper, more authentic identity rooted in the tradition and culture of the masses whom they represented. Resolution of this conflict was rendered more difficult since the pull of the foreign model was greater than the attraction presented by the indigenous one. This meant in effect a re-enforcement of western elitist tendencies rather than those emanating from the masses. When and how the traditional past will meet with the modern present to produce an authentic identity is the dilemma of the *awlād al-balad*, and perhaps this is also the main crisis of Egyptians in the twentieth century.

NOTE ON METHODOLOGY

Data for this essay has been compiled by several techniques. The main ones being content analysis of literary and historical sources, and field research. In order to ascertain how the concept *ibn al-balad* developed, an attempt was made to trace it back through literary, historical and folklore sources. Relevant folklore sources such as Sirat al-Ẓahir Baybars, 'Alī al-Zaybak, Sulaymān al-Habla and the Arabian Nights were reviewed, as well as the Goha stories, Egyptian proverbs and ballads. Relevant historical works were mainly the few which refer to the Egyptian society and in particular to common people, such as those by Ibn Iyas, al-Maqrizi, and al-Jabartī'. In reviewing the historical sources I limited myself to those using the epithet *ibn al-balad* or its derivative explicitly. The exploratory research in historical references showed that al-Jabartī's book, *'Aja' ib al-Athār fi'l-Tarājim wa'l-Akhbār* is rich in specific references to *ibn al-balad.* Hence I concentrated mainly on Jabartī's classical work. The relevant literary sources varied from autobiographies (*The Memories of a Futūwa*), to the novels of the contemporary novelist Nagīb Maḥfūz, to the classical first modern attempt at writing an Egyptian novel – *Ḥadīth 'Īsā ibn Ḥishām* by al-Muwaylihi.

Field research was carried out during numerous periods of varying length from the year 1968 to 1974. The main techniques for field research were participant observation and intensive interviews. To get at the life style of *awlād al-balad* the author participated in daily routine activities and in special events such as visiting saints and tombs, attending *mūlids* (festivals to celebrate the birthday of a saint), marriage cerenomies, funerals, etc. Part of the method of participant observation and interviewing was group discussion which emerged from the unique field situation of that group, i.e. *awlād al-balad.*

Transliteration in this book has been done according to the International Journal of Middle East Studies adapted to colloquial Egyptian usage.

GLOSSARY

abū: father
abukatū: lawyer
abwāb: military barracks of Janissary corps
'afūf: integrity
ahl al-balad: people of the country or town or village
ahl miṣr: people of Egypt or Cairo
akh: brother
al-agnād al-miṣrīyya: the Egyptian soldiers
al-aḥyā' al-sha'bīyya: folk quarters
al-'āmma: commoners
al-a'yān: notables
al-'uyyāq: outlaws
al-'uyyār: outlaws
al-Azhar: center for religious and university education; old center
al-baladī yawkal: baladi is edible, good
al-ghawghā': mob
al-ḥarāfīsh: rabble, riff-raff
al-ḥifūf: the process of depilation
al-ḥiraf al-dunya: low status crafts
al-jihād: holy war in Islam
al-khāssa: special people
al-mamalīk al-miṣrīyya: Egyptian Mamluks
al-miṣrī effendī: petty Egyptian bureaucrat
al-nās: the people
al-shuṭṭār: the clever
shuṭṭār (pl)., *shāṭir* (sing): now this term is commonly used denoting a clever man who knows how to get his way
al-sūqa: populace
al-tujjār: merchants
al-umarā' al-miṣrīyya: Egyptian princes
amīr: prince (*p. umarā'*)
amīr al-ḥajj: commander of the pilgrimage
andīl: lamp
arbāb al-ṣanā'i': craftsmen
ardhāl al-'āmma: riff-raff of the common people
'arusūs: local syrup or drink
arzāqi: one who earns his living day by day
ashrāf: descendants of the prophet (see Footnote 6, Chapter 1)
aṣīl: good stock, lineage
'atfā: narrow alley closed at the end
atbā': followers
awbāsh al-'āmma: riff-raff of the common people
awlād al-balad: (see *ibn al-balad*)
awlād al-zawāt: upper class persons
awlād miṣr: sons of Egypt or Cairo
awlīyā: saints
'azwa (*'aza*): one who has many supporters

baḥrāwi: from lower Egypt
balad: locality of any size
baladī: adjective derived from *balad*, i.e. local

ballāna: one who does depilation
baltāgī: thug
baraka: blessing
bayt 'ezz: prestigeous house
bayt maftūḥ: open house
bey: honorary title of address
bint al-balad: daughter of the country
bint al-sūq: daughter of the market, i.e. working in trade
bulgha: a yellow slipper

Daftardār: Mamluk chancellor
dallāla: woman seller
darb: central branch of a *ḥāra*
dāya: midwife
Diwān: council

effendī, effendīyya: title of address mainly for bureaucrats

fahlawa, fahlāwī: cleverness, one who is clever
fallāḥ, fallāḥa (fem), *fallāhīn* (pl): peasant, farmer
farīk: green wheat
fūl (mudammis): cooked fava beans
futūwa, futūwāt (pl), *fatwana:* (see end of chapter 3), gallantry, youth

gad'a, ged'ān, gad'ana: lit. manly (see Chapter 2, p. 63)
gallābīyya: flowing gown
gawzat al-ṭīb: nutmeg
gazīya: gypsy dancer
ghandūra: beautiful
gōza: long-stemmed pipe

ḥāgg, ḥāgga: title of address for those who have made the pilgrimage to Mecca or to an elderly person

ḥalāwa ṭaḥīniyya: a kind of sweet made from sesame
ḥāra, ḥārāt (pl): quarter, section
ḥārat al-ḥuṣr: a *ḥāra* in Hussiniyya quarter
ḥasharāt: insects
ḥashīsh: drug derived from Cannabis (hemp), smoked in *goza* or cigarettes
ḥidi': clever
ḥitta, ḥitat (pl): locality

ibn al-balad: son of the country, literally (see note, p. 1)
ifrangī: foreign
iltizām: system of farm tax (see nootnote 13 , chapter 1)

jubba: long outer garment
jūkha: overcoat only worn by the rich

kafya: a special kind of joking
kāshifs: intendants (see footnote 4, chapter 1)
katukhda: officer of the military corps, lieutenant to the Aga
khalīj: Gulf
khawāga, khawāgāt (pl): foreigner(s)
kuftan: type of robe or dress

kuḥl: powdered black antimony used for eye make-up
kuttāb: traditional school for teaching religion as well as reading and writing

līfa: natural sponge derived from gourd fibre

maghṭas: tub
maḥāsīb: followers or supporters
mahr: dowry
mara': woman (abusive)
mashādīd: those who stand for someone; supporters
mitfanaṭa: classified
miṣriyīn: Egyptians
milāya laff: square black overwrap for women
mish: very salty cheese
Miṣr: Egypt or Cairo
Miṣri: Egyptian
midardaḥ: alert, active (f. *midardaha*)
mitfarnaga: relative adjective of *ifrangi* (foreign)
mu'allim, mu'allima (fem): title of address referring to a chief man or woman.
muftī: the person in Islam who gives opinions (*fatwa*) on *Shari'a*, and its legislation
multazīm: he who holds an *iltizām* (see footnote 13, Chapter 1)
mūlid: birthday of a saint
murūwa: manliness, gallantry

naqīb: representative or marshal
niṣf: an Egyptian coin
nuqūṭ: money gifts

ojāq: (see *wijaq*)
osmalis: an adjective referring to all that is Turkish

pasha: honorary title of address for aristocrats; it was used to address the Turkish Governor of Egypt during the Ottoman Empire

qādī: chief judge
qā'im maqām: acting viceroy

rabāba: local musical instrument
ra'īya: subject masses
riwāq: an alley in a mosque used as a classroom; a class in al-Azhar
rizq: what God assigns to one as wealth
rūznāmijī: directory of scribes of the Treasury

ṣa'īdī: Upper Egyptian
sanjaq al-khazna: guardian of Port revenues
sha'b: people
shabka: betrothal gift
shahāma; shahm: gallantry, quality of gallantry; gallant
sharī'a: Islamic law
shaykh: an honorary title of address usually applied to the religious scholars. It also designates an older man
shaykh al-balad: local governor or headman of a village
shilla: clique
shīsha: water pipe, hookah
sitt: lady
siyar: biographies

subū‘: seventh day after birth of child; celebration of that day
subyān: lads, boys

ṭablīya: low round table
ṭa‘mīya: fried balls of ground beans and vegetables
ṭaqīya: headdress
takyīs: rubbing the body with a woollen cloth
tarbūsh: the head cover introduced by the Turks
tawāshih: classical arabic songs

‘ūd: oriental stringed instrument
umm: mother
‘umda: mayor
‘usab: bands, gangs
’usṭā: a title of address used now for workers or craftsmen, denoting expert
’uṣūl: traditional etiquette

wad: boy
waḥātīya: people from the oases
wālī: governor
wujāq, ojāq (pl): military corps

za‘būt: a brown woollen garment open from the neck nearly to the waist and having wide sleeves
zaffa: procession of the bride
zār: a ceremony and a class of spirits
zū’: taste, tact
zuqāq: alley
zu‘r: scoundrels

BIBLIOGRAPHY

Abd al-Karīm, A. Ezzat. "Ḥarakit al-Taḥāwul fi Binā' al-Mutjama' al-Qāhirī," *al-Mijala*, 149 (1969) pp. 50–55.

Abd al-Rahim, A. *al-Rīf al Misrī fi al-Qarn al-Thāmin-'Ashra*. al-Qāhira: Maṭābi' Gāmi'at Ain Shams, 1974.

Abu Lughod, Janet L. *Cairo: 1001 Years of the City Victorious*. Princeton, N.J.: Princeton University Press, 1971.

Abu Lughod, Ibrahim. "The Transformation of the Egyptian Elite: Prelude to the 'Urabi Revolt." *Middle East Journal*, Vol. XXI.

Amin, Ahmed. *Al-Sa'laka wa al-Futūwa fi al-Islām*. Miṣr: Dar al-Ma'arif, 1952.

Ammar, Hamed. *Fī Binā' al-Bashar*. Al-Qāhira: Community Development Center in the Arab World, Sirs al-Layyan, 1964.

Ayalon, D. "The Historian al-Jabartī and his Background," *Bulletin of the School of Oriental African Studies*, XXIII (1962), pp. 217–49.

Baer, Gabriel. "Social Change in Egypt: 1800–1914." *Political and Social Change in Modern Egypt*, pp. 135–161, edited by P.M. Holt. London: Oxford University Press, 1968.

al-Bīshrī, 'Abd al-'Azīz. "al-Effendi," *al-Thaqāfa*, 6, (1939) p. 21–22.

Breebart, D.A. "The Development and Structure of the Turkish Futuwwa Guilds," unpublished dissertation, Princeton, USA, 1961.

Fawzi, Hussīn. *Sindibād Miṣrī*. al-Qāhira: Dar al-Ma'arif, 1969.

Girgis, Fawzi. *Dirāsāt fi Tārīkh Miṣr al-Siyāsī Mundhu al-'Aṣr al-Mamlūkī*. al-Qāhira: Maṭba'at al-Dār al-Miṣriyya, 1958.

Gohar, M.H., M.A. el-Fatār. *Sirat al-Ẓāhir Baybars*. al-Qāhira: Dār al-Ma'arif 1968.

Hamady, Saniya. *Temperament and Character of the Arabs*. New York: Twayne Publishing Co., 1960.

El-Hamamsy, L. Shukry, "The Assertion of Egyptian Identity in Historical Perspective", unpublished paper presented to the Burg Wartenstein Symposium, No. 51, September 1970.

Haqqi, Yahya. *Qandīl Umm Ḥāshim*. al-Qāhira: Dar Al-Ma'ārif, 1954.

Hassanin, Fouad. *Al-Futūwa, ibn al-Mi'mar al-Baghdādy*. al-Qāhira: Dār al-Sha'b, 1959.

Hobsbawm, E.J. *Primitive Rebels*. (Studies in Archaic Forms of Social Movement in the 19th and 20th centuries) England: Manchester University Press, 1971.

Holt, P.M. (ed.) *Political and Social Change in Modern Egypt*. London: Oxford Univerisity Press, 1968.

Horney, K. "Symposium on Alienation and the Search for Identity." *American Journal of Psychoanalysis*, No. 21 (1961) pp. 117–279.

Ibn Iyās. *Badā'i' az-Zuhūr fī Waqā'i' ad-Duhūr*, 2 Vols. Cairo: (Būlaq) 1892. Vols. IV–V,2nd edition, edited by Muhammad Mustafā. Cairo: 1960–1961.

Issawi, Charles. "The Economic Development of Modern Egypt, 1800–1960," *The Economic History of the Middle East 1880–1914*, pp. 359–374, edited by Charles Issawi. Chicago and London: The University of Chicago Press, 1966.

al-Jabartī, *'Ajā'ib al-Āthār fi al-Tarājim wa-al-Akhbār*. First published in 1880, Qāhira: Matba't al-Sha'b edition 1958.

al-Jam'iyya al-Misriyya lil- Dirāsāt al-Ijtimā'īyya. *Dirāsa Ijtimā'īyya Lil khadamāt bi Hay Bab al-Sha'riyya*. al-Qāhira: Maktab al-Buḥūth al-ijtimā'iyya, 1965.

Dirāsa Ijtimā'iyya Lil-'usar wa al-khadamāt bi Hay al-Darb al-Aḥmar. al-Qāhira: Buḥūth al-ijtimā'īyya, 1958.

Dirasā Ijtimā'iyya Lil-khadarmat bi Hay al-Sayida Zaynab. al-Qāhira: Maktab al-Buhūth al-ijtimā'yya, 1958.

— *Dirasā Ijtimā'iyya Lil-'usar wa al-khadamāt bi Hay al-Darb al-Aḥmar*. al-Qāhira: Maktab al-Buḥūth al-ijtimā'īyya, 1970.
— *Dirasā Ijtimā'iyya Lil khadamāt bi Hay Miṣr al-Qādīmā*. al-Qāhira: Maktab al-Buḥūth al-ijtimā'īyya, 1957.
Jawad Mustafa, al-Halali M.T., al-Najjar A.B. *Kitab al-Futūwa L'ibn al-Mi'mār*. Baghdad: Matba't Baghdad, 1958.
Kennedy, John. "Mushahra, Nubian Concept of Supernatural Danger and the Theory of Taboo," *American Anthropologist*, Vol. 69, No. 6, (1967).
Khurshid, Farouq. *'Ali al-Ziybaq* al-Qāhira: Dār al-Hilāl, 1967.
Klapp, E. Orrin. *Heroes, Villains, and Fools: The Changing American Character*. New Jersey: Prentice Hall, Inc., 1962.
Lapidus, Ira M. *Muslim Cities in the Later Middle Ages*. Cambridge, Mass: University Press, 1967.
Lane, Edward W. *An Account of the Manners and Customs of the Modern Egyptians* (1836). 1860 edition, London: Everyman's Library, 1908.
Lane-Pole, Stanley. *Cairo, Sketches of its History, Monuments, and Social Life*. London, 1895.
Levy, Reuben. *The Social Structure of Islam*. London: Cambridge University Press, 1957.
Loutfi el-Sayed, Afaf. "The Role of the 'Ulama, in Egypt during the Early Nineteenth Century," *Political and Social Change in Modern Egypt, pp. 264–280,* edited by P. M. Holt. London: Oxford University Press, 1968.
Maccoby, E.E., Newcomb, M.T., Hartley, L.E. *Readings in Social Psychology*. New Jersey: Rinehart and Winston, Inc., 1958.
Mahfūz, Naguib. *al-Sukkariya*. al-Qāhira: Dār Miṣr, 1957.
—. *Qasr al-Shawq*. al-Qāhira: Dār Miṣr, 1957.
—. *Khān al-Khalīlī*. al-Qāhira: Dār Miṣr, 1965.
—. *Zuqāq al-Midaq*. al-Qāhira: Dār Miṣr, 1963.
—. *Bayn al-Qasrayn*. al-Qāhira: Dār Miṣr, 1964.
—. *Awlād Hāratna*. Beirut: Dar al-adab, 1972.
—. *Hikayāt Hāratna*. al-Qāhira: Maktabat Misr. 1975.
al-Maqrīzī. *'Ighāthat al-Umma bi Kashf al-Ghumma,* edited by Jamāl al-Din Muhammad ash-Shayyal and Muhammad Mustafa Ziyāda. Cairo: 1940.
Mayhew, Henry. *London Labour and the London Poor* (1851–64).
al-Miligi, Mahmoud. "Ḥadīth al-dhikrayāt," *al-Akhbār*, 10 December 1970.
Mubārak, 'Ali Pasha. *Al-Khiṭāt al-Tawfiqiyya al-Jadida li-Miṣr al-Qāhira*. 20 Vols. in 5. Cairo (Bulaq): 1888.
al-Muwaylihī, Muhammad. *Hadīth Isa Ibn Hishām*. al-Qāhira: Al-Dār al-Qawmiyya lil-Tibā'a wal-Nashīr 1964. First published in 1900.
el-Messiri, Sawsan. "The Changing Role of the Futuwa in the Social Structure of Cairo," *Patrons and Clients in the Mediterranean Societies*, edited by Ernest Gellner and John Waterbury. England: Duckworth Press, 1977.
Nadim, N. el-Messiri, *The Relationship Between the Sexes in a Harah of Cairo*. Unpublished Ph.D. dissertation. Department of Anthropology, Indiana University, 1975.
Natanson, Maurice, *Philosophy of the Social Sciences*. New York: Random House, 1963.
Niklawi, H. *A Social Study of Cairo*. Unpublished Ph.D. dissertation. Department of Sociology, Cairo University, 1970.
Owen, Roger. "Egypt and Europe: from French expedition to British Occupation." *Studies in the Theory of Imperialism*, edited by Roger Owen and Bob Sutcliffe. 1972.
Raymond, André. *Artisans et commerçants au Caire*, 2 Vols. Damascus: Institut Français, 1973, 1974.

—. "Les bains publiques au Caire à la fin du XVIIe siècle," *Annals Islamologiques*, VIII, pp. 129-150. Cairo: L'Institut Français d'Archéologie Orientale, 1969.

—. "Quartiers et mouvements populaires au Caire au XVIIIe siècle," *Political and Social Change in Modern Egypt,* pp. 104-116, edited by P.M. Holt. London: Oxford University Press, 1968.

Shadi, 'Alī. *'Ali al-Ziybaa al-Misrī.* Unpublished thesis, Cairo University, 1968.

Sha'lān H. Ibrahim. *al-Sha'b al-Miṣri Fī Amthāluh al-'āmīyya.* al-Qāhira: Maṭābi' al-Haya'a al-'Āmma lil-Kitāb, 1972.

Shaw, Stanford J. *The Financial and Administrative Organization and Development of Ottoman Egypt, 1517–1798.* Princeton, N.J.: University Press, New York.

el-Shayyal, Gamal al-Din. "Some Aspects of Intellectual and Social Life in Eighteenth century Egypt," *Political and Social Change in Modern Egypt,* pp. 117–132, edited by P.M. Holt. London: Oxford University Press, 1968.

Schutz, Alfred. *The Phenomenology of the Social World.* Translated by George Walsh and Frederick Lehnert.

Staffa, J. Susan. *Conquest and Fusion: The Social Evolution of Cairo, A.D. 642–1850.* Leiden: E.J. Brill, 1977.

Taymour, Ahmad. *al-Amthāl al-'Āmmiyya.* al-Qāhira: Dār al-Kitāb al-'Arabī, 1956.

Tomiche, Nada. "Notes sur la hiérarchie sociale en Égypte à l'époque de Muhammad 'Ali," *Political and Social Change in Modern Egypt,* pp. 249–263, edited by P. M. Holt. London: Oxford University Press, 1968.

al-Tunisī, Bayram. *Dīwān Bayram al-Tūnisī.* Misr: Dār al-Kitāb al-'Arabī, 1948.

—. *Maqāmāt Bayram.* Introduction by Tāhir Abou Fashā. al-Qāhira: Maktabat Madbūlī, 1973.

—. *Alā Bāb al-Jāmī'.* al-Qāhira: Maktabat Madbūlī, 1974.

'Uwas, Sayyid. *Malamiḥ al-Mujtama' al-Mīṣri al-Mū'āṣir* (Zāhirat irsāl al-rasā'il 'ilā dārih al-Imām al-Shāfi'i). al-Qāhira': Dār wa Maṭābi' al-Sha'b, 1965.

—. *Hitāf al-Sāmitīn* (Zāhirat al-Kitāba 'āla Ḥyākil al-Markabāt fi al-Mujtama' al-Miṣri al-Mu'āṣir). al-Qāhira: Dār al-Tibā'a al-Hadītha, 1971.

Wahida, Soubhi. *Fi Usūl al-Mas'ala al-Misriyya.* al-Qāhira: Matba'at Misr, 1950.

Wali al-Din, Isma'īl. *Hamam al-Malatili.* al-Qahira: Kitābāt Mu'āṣira, 1970.

Weber, Max. *Sociology of Religion.* Boston: Beacon Press, 1969.

Yūnis, Abd al-Hamīd. "Ibn al-Balad: Shakhsiyyatuh wa Ikhlāqiyyatuh" *al-Fūnun al-sha'biyya* (1965).

Yūsif, al-Haggāg. *Mudhakkarāt Futūwa.* al-Qāhira: 1927.

INDEX